RONNIE MCDOWELL
BRINGING IT TO YOU PERSONALLY

THE AUTOBIOGRAPHY
WITH SCOT ENGLAND

*"I've done everything I ever wanted to do. I've had my day in the sun...
and it was as bright as I dreamed it would be. How many people can say that?"*
- Ronnie McDowell

Ronnie McDowell
Bringing It To You Personally

The Autobiography

Copyright © England Media 2015
102 Rachels Ct Hendersonville TN 37075
(615) 804-0361
englandmedia@yahoo.com
ronniemcdowellbook.com
All rights reserved.

Editor: Lindsey McNealy
Cover Design: Paula Underwood Winters
Internal Design: Steve Williams, Red Inc
Cover Photo: Dennis Carney Photo Imaging
Back Cover Photo: Mike Payne

ISBN 978-0-692-57268-9

Printed by Jostens, Clarksville TN 37040

Dedication

This book is dedicated to my sweet mother.
I also dedicate it to my father... to my children, and to my grandchildren...
to God, for allowing me to live my dream.
And to all the wonderful fans who have been there for almost 40 years.

Contents

Foreword by George Klein 9

Foreword by Ray Walker 11

Chapter One - August 17, 1977 13

Chapter Two - Georgia On My Mind 15

Chapter Three - Angel On My Shoulder 19

Chapter Four - You Look Just Like Elvis... (If Elvis had green hair and chipped teeth) . 24

Chapter Five - Most Talented... But Not For Singing 25

Chapter Six - In The Navy 27

Chapter Seven - Karen 31

Chapter Eight - Beaten By A Ballerina 33

Chapter Nine - Songwriting, Singing… and Scorpions 35

Chapter Ten - The King Is Gone 37

Chapter Eleven - Fame... But Not Much Fortune 43

Chapter Twelve - Life… And Death 45

Chapter Thirteen - The Voice Of Elvis 47

Chapter Fourteen - We Want Elvis! But Does Anyone Want Ronnie? 51

Chapter Fifteen - News Flash: Billy Graham Loves Older Women! 53

Chapter Sixteen - Conway 55

Chapter Seventeen - How To Lose A Million Dollars... Twice 61

CHAPTER EIGHTEEN - The Headhunters 63

CHAPTER NINETEEN - Mom Always Said To Wear Clean Underwear In Case...
(A few of my most memorable road experiences) 65

CHAPTER TWENTY - Eve Said To Adam... "Clothes don't make the man." 77

CHAPTER TWENTY-ONE - The Truth 81

CHAPTER TWENTY-TWO - My Kids 83

CHAPTER TWENTY-THREE - The Tornado Was Trying To Tell Me Something. 85

CHAPTER TWENTY-FOUR - Jamie 87

CHAPTER TWENTY-FIVE - "Yes, He Is Your Kid" 89

CHAPTER TWENTY-SIX - My Musical Family 91

CHAPTER TWENTY-SEVEN - My Fans... My Friends 105

CHAPTER TWENTY-EIGHT - Truth Is Stranger Than Fiction 109

CHAPTER TWENTY-NINE - My Elvis Family 111

CHAPTER THIRTY - Never Fly Off The Handle 119

CHAPTER THIRTY-ONE - Here's Your Sign 121

CHAPTER THIRTY-TWO - The Hits... And A Couple That Should Have Been . 125

CHAPTER THIRTY-THREE - Didn't You Used To Be...? 131

CHAPTER THIRTY-FOUR - I'm Going To Disneyland! 133

CHAPTER THIRTY-FIVE - Friends 135

CHAPTER THIRTY-SIX -
    If Older Women Are Better... Older Men Need To Stay Healthy! .. 145

CHAPTER THIRTY-SEVEN - Parting Song By Scot England 149

Foreword

I had just lost my best friend. My best friend Elvis Presley.

Elvis and I had been best friends since we were classmates at Hume High School.

I was part of Elvis' small inner circle, dubbed by many as the "Memphis Mafia". We were so close that Elvis was Best Man at my wedding. It was the one and only time Elvis ever stood up as Best Man at someone's wedding.

But a short time after Elvis died, another person came into my life.

Charlie Hodge, who was also one of Elvis' closest friends, told me that I needed to meet a country artist named Ronnie McDowell. Charlie said, "This guy sounds so much like Elvis that it is scary. But he is not an Elvis impersonator."

So I went to see Ronnie in concert. We met after the show, and that was the start of a great friendship that has now lasted almost four decades.

A short time after we first met, I started working with the casinos in Tunica, Mississippi. And I told my bosses that they should book Ronnie McDowell. They did, and he has been playing Tunica ever since.

For more than 40 years, every Christmas I put on a huge charity concert in Memphis. One year I asked Ronnie to be on the show. He was on the bill with a long list of other great performers. On the afternoon of the concert, he called and said his bus had broken down in Alabama.

But he said "I am not missing your show."

And Ronnie and his entire band ended up buying plane tickets to fly to Memphis.

When they got there, I wanted to reimburse his expenses, and he absolutely refused. He paid it all, and did the concert with all of the money going to my charity.

Ronnie was never an Elvis impersonator. He never tried to look or act like Elvis. He never wore a white jumpsuit. But he became known as "The Voice of Elvis". He reminds me a whole lot of Elvis… not only because he sounds like Elvis, but because he is such a nice guy. He is so polite to people. Ronnie treats his fans so good. He signs autographs and takes pictures. He gives of his time.

He is one of the nicest entertainers I have ever met. And I have met them all.

I love you Ronnie.

George Klein

George Klein
Charter Member, Elvis' Memphis Mafia.

Foreword

It seems like I have known Ronnie McDowell forever. Ronnie is one of the best friends I've got. He connected to my heart from the moment we first met.

I became a member of The Jordanaires in 1958. I started working with Ronnie McDowell almost two decades later. I love to hear Ronnie laugh. He has the best laugh of anyone in the world. He loves to laugh, and I always try to make him laugh when we are on stage. There have been many times when he has told me, "You are just not right!"

He once introduced The Jordanaires on stage and said, "You guys have been around a long time." I asked him, "How long do you think we've been singing?" He said, "Well, that depends." I looked at him and yelled, "Don't you have sense enough to know that you should never say the word 'Depends' to men who are over 80 years old?!" Ronnie fell to his knees laughing!

Ronnie is the most unusual person I have ever met. He is working all the time. When he's not on stage, he's writing, or building something, or painting. And his paintings are absolutely beautiful. He is busy all the time.

Ronnie is so loved by everyone who works with him. And none more than me. You've heard of people who are joined at that hip? Ronnie and I are joined at the heart.

In the Bible, Jesus says, "There is a friend that sticks closer than a brother"... and that is Ronnie McDowell.

Ray Walker
The Jordanaires.

Chapter One

August 17, 1977

I am so close. So close.

We are just five feet away!

I had missed my chance to see Elvis when he was alive. But at least now I would see him as I said "Goodbye".

After hearing that Elvis had died, me and my friend Bill Huntsman drove from Portland Tennessee to Memphis. We had driven my '77 Camaro as fast as we could the entire way.

For the past ten hours, we have been crammed in the middle of tens of thousands of mourning Elvis fans. We had all converged on the gates of Graceland. For the past twenty years, fans had come to these gates in hopes of getting a glimpse of Elvis. Today, we are here one final time for the same reason.

But the combination of raw grief and the August Memphis heat and humidity is too much for many in the crowd. We have watched as one person after another has collapsed, as the temperature hit 100 degrees.

For more than three hours, the Presley family has opened Graceland's gates to Elvis' fans, so they can walk up the long driveway and step into the home. There they file past Elvis' open casket.

And now I am so close! Just five feet from going inside the gate.

But the gates begin to shut. The guards push back the surging, and now desperate, crowd. The public visitation has been stopped.

We don't get in.

My chance to see Elvis is gone forever.

As I watch the gates to Graceland close... I have no idea that, in the years ahead, I will be inside those gates as an invited guest.

As Elvis' family mourns his death... I could not dream that, in the years to come, I will get to know his wife Priscilla, and many of his family members, personally.

As Elvis' band and entourage members think about their future without him... I would never imagine that I will work alongside almost all of them.

As Elvis' closest friends suffer on this hot August day in 1977... I could never believe that I will become a close friend of theirs.

As we got into our car to start our long drive back home, I tell Bill, "Ya know, I was barely six years old when I first heard him sing..."

I never got to see Elvis in person... but in less than a week, he will change my life forever.

Chapter Two

Georgia On My Mind

Georgia Mae McDowell... my mother was the best person who ever lived... spiritually and morally. There was nobody like my mother.

Mother was born in 1919. She was married when she was 13 years old! Daddy was 21. My parents married in 1933 on a porch in Portland, Tennessee. Elmer Henton married them for $2.25. Daddy handed him $2.50, and Mr. Henton told him that was too much.

They went to Florida for a honeymoon, and they stopped at the Eastland Hotel in Chattanooga. Remember, my mom was only 13! The next morning, they got off the elevator and the bellboy asked my dad "Sir, did you and your little girl sleep good last night?"

My parents ended up having 10 kids. Nine of those lived, but we always counted my little sister, too. My mom was 9 months pregnant when she fell off a porch. It killed the baby. My parents named that baby girl Priscilla. Another Priscilla would become a part of my life years later.

On March 25, 1950, Ronald Dean McDowell was born at Highland Hospital in Portland, Tennessee. Highland was the county hospital. Out of the eleven kids in our family, I am the 7th from the bottom. There were three younger than me. It was great growing up with a big family. All my family, all my brothers and sisters, have stayed real close through the years.

At the time of my birth, my parents nor their doctors knew that I had a genetic disorder. I had inherited Alpha 1 antitrypsin deficiency. That is a weakness of the lungs. It also harms your blood and liver. When I was just a few days old, I began turning black and blue. When you have that disease, you are not able to make green bile from your liver. My oldest sister Caroline was 13 years old, and she helped get me to the hospital.

After examining me, Doctor Johnson, the doctor who had birthed me, said I was not going to make it through the night. He had given up on me. My fingernails had already turned blue, and I was turning black from a lack of oxygen.

Later that night, my grandmother Avis (we always called her Mama) came to the hospital and brought some sheets. She said "We can wrap the baby up in these when he dies." My sister went off on my grandma. She yelled, "Take those sheets back home. He is not going to die!"

A short time later, Caroline saw an old Indian woman walk in the room. She raised the window up and she told my sister to massage my chest. The Indian woman knew I was not getting oxygen.

The next morning, my color had started coming back. When the doctor came in, he said, "This is a miracle! I thought this child would be gone."

It was a miracle. And I did survive. But that horrible Alpha 1 antitrypsin deficiency would strike the McDowell family once again, many years down the road.

In the 1940s, Daddy built and ran a beer joint right on the Kentucky/Tennessee state line. The building is still there today. But one night, mother took a cab out to the business and she caught Dad with another woman. She caught him red-handed, right in the beer joint.

My mother and father divorced in 1955, when I was 5 years old.

My dad's infidelity was the cause for their marriage trouble.

My parent's divorce affected my older brothers and sister in a big way. They had a lot of bitterness toward my dad.

As for me… I became one sad, lonely little kid.

I cried all the time. I cried so much that my mother sent me to live with my big sisters in Nashville. But I cried so much there that they sent me to live with my sister in St Louis. I was 11 years old, and they put me on a bus all by myself!

I just wanted to be with my dad. And once I got that chance, my dad and I became good buddies. On most Saturdays, my dad would come take me and my brothers to the movies up in Franklin, Kentucky. We would stay at the movies all day. He would take us to a little diner called The Wagon Wheel. I would eat buckwheat pancakes and chocolate milk.

But it was my mother who really had to raise us all.

And we were poor.

At times, mother was working three different jobs, trying to take care of ten kids. She worked in different restaurants. She worked real hard.

Imagine the stress of trying to feed, clothe and care for ten kids on your own! Most nights, she slept just sitting in a chair. She worked very hard, right up until I had the hit "The King Is Gone". I made her life easier after I had that record. I always said, if I had any success, I would let her live a life of luxury, and that's exactly what I did.

I am glad that I am a child of the 50s. To me, the 50s were the most gentle times.

Times were so simple back in the 1950s. There was only one policeman in Portland. His name was Wilson Brown. When he would go home for lunch, there wouldn't be any police in town!

The world was just different back then. It was a beautiful time. The music was beautiful. If I could live any decade over, it would be the 50s.

I loved the 1950s. But I did not love school. I hated it. When I was in the first grade, I played hooky 36 times! Why my teacher passed me, I will never know.

But I made sure that I was in school at Christmas time. Every Christmas, the school would give us a little brown paper bag. That bag was filled with an apple, an orange, two walnuts and one peppermint stick. What a treat that was!

With our family being so poor, I learned the value of hard work at a very early age. When I was little, the Consumer's Drug Store had a contest. In the window, they had all these prizes you could win. I was always there with my nose pressed up against the window, looking at those prizes. It was just like that scene in the movie "A Christmas Story" when Ralphie is looking at that Red Ryder BB gun. But I didn't want a BB gun. One of the prizes at the drug store was a model airplane. And I wanted that plane so bad. You won the prizes by collecting store receipts. So every day after school, I would stand out in front of that store, asking people for their receipts. The contest ended on Christmas Eve, and all my hard work paid off when I was the winner of that airplane! I walked home with it and I almost broke it, I was hugging it so tight.

Not far from the drug store was a laundromat. It had a sign on the front that said, "Whites Only". I asked my mother "Why do they only wash white clothes? Why can't they do blue and red clothes?" Mother whispered, "Ronnie, that is not what that sign means."

Chapter Three

Angel On My Shoulder

Singing is all I ever wanted to do. How many people can say that that they knew what they wanted to do when they were four years old? I can.

At the age of four, I was walking around the house singing Hank Williams. My earliest memory is sitting on the back porch singing "Your Cheating Heart" and "Lovesick Blues." And even at that very young age, I could do that little yodel that Hank did.

My sister Linda Sue would bring home great records from Randy's Record Shop in Gallatin, Tennessee, right down the road from where we lived. She'd buy those and I would listen to them and I would emulate everyone, every voice I heard. We listened to Hank Williams, Johnny Cash, Sam Cooke, The Platters, Louie Armstrong, Lefty Frizzell, Fats Domino, Little Richard. I loved everybody. I have an eclectic group of artists who influenced me.

In 1954, Linda Sue brought a big 78 record home. It was Elvis Presley's "That's All Right Mama" on Sun Records. When I heard that, it was like someone poured a bucket of water on me! And I found out that out of all of my favorites, Elvis was the easiest for me to sound like.

When I was six years old, I saw Elvis on the Tommy Dorsey Show on TV. And my first thought was "How can he sing like that and look like that…he is too pretty to be a guy." From then on, I was Elvis crazy. I listened to his songs constantly. I learned every nuance, every syllable, every bend of the note that he did.

In 1958, my mother had a big Philco radio. It was one of those big ole, tall wooden radios. That radio looked huge when I was a little boy. Every day I had my ears glued to it. Every day, all day long. Mother would get mad at me for listening so much. But I just loved music.

While I loved to sing around the house, I would never sing in public. I was always very, very shy. I was painfully shy. I would never sing in front of people. But I would go out in the woods with a little tape recorder and I would sing my heart out. I was so shy. Today, if I see a kid who is painfully shy, I talk to them. I tell them it is OK to be that way. But I try to get them to come out of that shell.

While mother was trying to provide a good home for all of her kids, my dad was building homes. Dad built homes for resale in Portland in the 40s and 50s. Most of those houses cost $12,500 when they were first sold, and most of them are still great homes today. And they sell for much more than $12,500, more than 60 years after they were built!

My grandfather died when I was nine. He was my mother's dad. And they brought his body to his home. That was the custom back then. They didn't keep the body at a funeral home like they do today. Friends and neighbors would come to the home to pay their respects, and the body would be there. I went with my mom, and she said we were going to stay the night at my grandparent's home the night before the funeral. That entire night, I wouldn't go to sleep because I thought my grandpa was going to come out of that casket to get me!

But I almost ended up in a casket in August of 1958.

I was nine years old. Me and my two brothers were walking down Lake Springs Road in Franklin, Kentucky, not far from where we lived.

It was a dark night. As we walked, we could feel someone watching us.

All of the sudden, rifle shots filled the air. My brother fell to the ground. He had been hit. One of the bullets hit him in the back and came out his stomach. Blood was everywhere. As I looked at him on the ground, another blast rang out. I was hit in the right side of my neck. It threw me out into the middle of the road.

We laid there, thinking we were probably going to die on that dark road. But a couple minutes later, two girls drove up and put us in their car. As they sped to the hospital, Jack Pruett, a Portland policeman, pulled us over. When he saw all the blood on us, he gave us a high speed escort to the hospital.

The doctors said it was a miracle that the bullet that passed through my brother's back and stomach, did not hit any major organ. And the doctor said if the bullet that hit me in the neck would have been over just a quarter of an inch, it would have hit my jugular vein and instantly killed me.

He said, "You guys must have had an angel on your shoulder, knocking those bullets away from you."

Later, the cops arrested a man named Gene Hodges. He had shot us with a .22 caliber rifle. During his trial, his lawyer put me on the stand. The lawyer had a seersucker suit on. He got right in my face and said, "Is it not true, that you and your brothers were going through this man's house and fooling around with his wife?"

I started crying. The judge told the lawyer, "I can't believe you would talk to this child like that."

They gave Gene Hodges two years in prison. After he got out, someone shot and killed him.

Chapter Four

You Look Just Like Elvis...
(If Elvis had green hair and chipped teeth)

Me and one of my best friends Rex Graves would go see every Elvis movie as soon as it was released. When we were in our mid teens, Rex told me that he wished he had dark black hair like Elvis. I told him I could help him get that black hair. I had actually bought the black hair color for myself, but I thought it might be good to have someone else try it out first!

Before school one morning, Rex came over and I put this black rinse on his hair. It wasn't really a dye. It was a rinse of some kind. And it looked real good as we started walking to school. Rex said, "Man I look like Elvis." But by the time we got to school, Rex's hair had turned as green as grass. It was bright green!

A short time after that, we went to another Elvis movie. And Rex said, "I wish I had pearly white teeth like Elvis." I said, "Hey I have ordered this stuff that will give you white teeth. I found it in the back of a magazine."

As soon as it came in the mail, Rex came over and I put it on his teeth. It was a whitener. And once again, when Rex started off to school, he looked great. His teeth were sparkling, they were so white. He couldn't stop smiling. But just an hour or so later, that whitening stuff started to chip off and it looked like all of his teeth were dark and broken!

When I was fourteen, I sent a letter to Graceland. I addressed the envelope, "Elvis Presley, Graceland, Memphis, TN. In the letter I wrote, "Hey Elvis, if you ever need somebody who sounds exactly like you, please let me know." I never got a response!

A year later I turned from writing fan letters to Elvis to writing love letters to my first girlfriend. I met Marsha Bradley when I was 15 years old. She was 13. Marsha was my first true love. We were like two peas in a pod. Marsha and I stayed very close through my high school years. I really loved her.

In 1965, me and a friend hitchhiked to Madison, Tennessee, where Colonel Parker had his office. My sister worked at the telephone office in Madison, and she would call and tell me when Elvis was in town. He would stay at the Anchor Motel, which is gone now. He would also stay at the Colonel's house. Colonel Tom had a place in the back fixed up just for Elvis. So my sister called, and me and a buddy hitchhiked to Madison to try to meet Elvis. We got there and we walked down the driveway. We opened the door, and there was a huge poster that said, "Elvis in Double Trouble". It was one of his movie posters. We knew we had hit pay dirt! But right then, a guard came running up, yelling "Hey you kids, get out here!" And we did. We should have stuck around.

That same year, I worked at the Miller Goads Texico station in Portland. They paid me $3.00 a day. It was at that filling station that I once bought a special gift.

It was just before Christmas, and me and my friend Rex were walking through town. They were playing Christmas songs on the speakers all over Portland. We walked through town, listening to the music as the snow was gently falling. It really was like a scene in "It's A Wonderful Life".

After thinking about what would be the perfect present for Rex, I went to the Miller Goad gas station and bought the world's largest peppermint stick. It was a foot long and a couple inches wide. I gave it to Rex, and when I went to his house two days later, he had already ate the whole thing!

And can you believe that Rex kept the original box that peppermint stick came in. He still has it today, 50 years later! I had signed it, "To Rex, my very best friend."

When I think of Rex, I think of candy. He liked candy. When we were fifteen years old, we were out driving in my dad's truck. Rex got a bag of jelly beans and was eating them as I drove. We went around this curve and the door flew open and he fell out. I looked in the rear view mirror and he was sitting in the road, and he still had a hold on those jelly beans! We were so lucky that I didn't run over his head and kill him.

Chapter Five

Most Talented... But Not For Singing

When I wasn't inside listening to music, or inside the theater watching Elvis movies, I was outside playing some kind of sport. I played every sport there was. I played baseball, basketball, football, and any other sport we could come up with.

When I was fifteen years old, I was playing football and I broke my third vertebrae. One of my friends accidentally stepped on my back and you could hear it pop all over the football field. So I had to lay on my back on a piece of plywood for two weeks at Highland Hospital. That's the Seventh Day Adventist Hospital in Portland where I was born. While I was recovering there, they started bringing me tofu food. I had never heard of it before, but I absolutely loved it. When people ask me today how I have stayed slim and physically fit all my life, I give a lot of the credit to that early love of tofu food.

As an athlete, I was O.K. on the playing field. But as a student, I was almost expelled from the classroom. School was the last thing on my mind. I couldn't care less about school. I graduated. But I didn't apply myself to my studies too much.

But even with my lack of effort, I was still voted the "Most Talented" of our class. That was for sports, and for my art, because I hadn't started singing in public yet. My sophomore year, all my friends wanted me to run for Class Vice President. But you had to have at least a C average. When I became Vice President, I had all C's, but six weeks later, when I didn't keep my grades up, they kicked me out of being Vice President!

All of my family members had nicknames. My nickname was Gunga Din. My sister, Linda Sue...we called her Tutti. She loved Little Richard's song "Tutti Frutti."

I have the sweetest, most loving, kindest sisters. They have supported me all my life.

While mother was working three jobs, trying to support ten kids, Daddy was dreaming… and working toward those dreams. In 1967 when I was seventeen, I found Daddy sitting, looking at a vacant field.

He was a visionary. And I know that I inherited much of my "dream big" attitude and goal setting from my dad. As he looked at the empty field, I asked him what he was doing. He said, "Son, I am going to put a store here." Back then, there was nothing at all there, but he built "Dixie Discount". It was a great little store. I worked in the store and I sold little potted flower plants for a dollar.

But life was about to get a lot more complicated. I would soon be trading Dixie Discount for the Tonkin Gulf, off the coast of Vietnam.

Chapter Six

In The Navy

Like millions of other teenage boys in the 1960s, I started closely following the nightly news... as my 18th birthday got closer.

In 1968, I thought if I joined the Navy, I wouldn't have to go to Vietnam. But right after I joined, I got a big ole manila envelope in the mail that said "Vietnam"!

Before I went into the Navy, I went to say goodbye to my best friend Rex Graves and his parents. And as I drove off, Rex's dad was crying like a baby. His family loved me that much. And I loved all of them.

I had boot camp in San Diego. My friend Larry McCall, from Columbia, Tennessee, went into boot camp with me. We had two days off from camp, and Larry and I went to the Fillmore West in San Francisco. We watched Janis Joplin sing "Take a Little Piece of My Heart." Even though I wasn't into that type of music, I was really awestruck by her voice.

The next day, we went to see them again. They were at Berkley with Jefferson Airplane. We went to the show and we weren't there 15 or 20 minutes and all of the women started taking their tops off! We had never seen anything like that... and we were in hog heaven!

But that heaven was short lived as we left Clark Air Force Base. We headed to the Philippines, loaded in a mail plane. When we got there, we landed on the USS Hancock. They had a grappling hook that caught us when we landed. And as soon as we arrived, Larry McCall started throwing up. He got seasick immediately.

While Larry was getting seasick, I was about to get heartsick.

In 1953 Ferlin Husky and Jean Shepard had a big hit with the song called 'Dear John'. It was about a soldier who received a letter from his girlfriend back home. She was writing to tell him she would not be waiting for him when he came home because she was seeing another man.

The song was a hit because thousands of soldiers and military men had received that same 'Dear John' letter.

Well, as soon as I arrived in Vietnam, I got a letter from my high school love Marsha Bradley. I can still remember that orange envelope. I was so excited to open it to see how much Marsha had missed me! But as soon as I took the letter out, I read the first two words..."Dear John". I turned the envelope over and it was addressed to Ronnie McDowell. But in the letter, Marsha actually wrote "Dear John"!

I wanted to laugh. But I couldn't. My 18 year old heart was broken. My first true love was over.

The USS Hancock was stationed just outside Saigon. And we went back and forth as they shot the planes off the ship.

I was in the Navy from 1968 to 1972, and I ended up being a combat veteran in 1968, 69 and 72. I started my hitch in the Navy in Vietnam. After a couple of years, I was sent to Adak, Alaska, and then in 1972 I was sent back to Vietnam.

All that time, I had been studying real hard, and I made E-5 Petty Officer -2nd Class. That's hard to do in 4 years, but I worked hard. Making E-5 upped my pay scale. When I got to Vietnam, I was working on the deck force. Someone asked if there was anyone good at art who could paint a sign. I volunteered, and I made them the best sign they had ever seen. I still have that sign in all my Navy stuff.

But when they learned I was E-5, they asked me what I wanted to do. I had found out that the best and easiest job on the ship was to be a barber. So I told them, "I would like to be a barber." They asked, "You can cut hair?" I said, "Of course I can." I had never cut hair in my life! But in less than two weeks, I was so good at it that I got a job cutting hair in the officer's shop.

One day, one of the Admirals came up to me. His name was Admiral Morrison. He told me he was headed to get his son out of jail. I asked him what happened. The Admiral told me his son "had showed his privates while he was on stage". His son had been arrested for being obscene during a concert. His son was Jim Morrison of The Doors!

It was during my time in the Navy that I started to act on a burning desire that I had carried with me since I was a child. I wanted to be an entertainer. And I wanted to write and sing songs.

One day, we took R and R in Olangapo City, in the Subek Bay of the Philippines. I was eighteen years old. I had never had a drop of alcohol. Me and Larry McCall went to a club called The Playboy Club. I had one beer… it was called a San Miguel beer… and after drinking that beer, all of my shyness just went away. I told Larry, "I'm going to get up there and sing." Larry said, "You are going to do what?"

But I went up and asked the band if they could knew any Elvis songs. They said they knew "It's Now Or Never"… and that was the very first time that I sang on stage in front of anyone.

And if I say so myself, I was dead on it. I had Elvis down already… and this is the God's truth… every girl in the club rushed that stage! They called all of us "Joe". And they came up to me and said, "Joe, let me take you home tonight. Please Joe, let me take you home." Right then I knew that was all I wanted to do for the rest of my life!

I got me a guitar, and during our down time, me and two other guys would go around singing. During a break in the fighting, they had a talent show. Me and my friends Joe Hedgepath and Chuck Nitche did an Elvis song. We did "When My Blue Moon Turns To Gold Again." Just before we went on, an old man grabbed me and said, "Elvis Presley stood right there where you are going to sing." He said, "I was here when Elvis was." He was. Elvis had played on the USS Hancock on the Milton Berle Show in 1956.

After I was sent from Vietnam to Alaska, I formed a band called "Ronnie Dean and the Remanences." We played in the Officers' Club on Friday night, and the Enlisted Club on Saturday night. We got $50 bucks a night. That was big money for a sailor back then… tax-free.

The first thing I ever recorded was in Adak, Alaska in 1971. There was a church there, and me and a friend would go in the church when they were not having services, because the echo in there was unbelievable. We set up our recorder, and I had written two songs. And as soon as we had finished, the priest came in and said, "Son, this is not a church of secular music and you can't sing that type of music in here." I said, "Well, we already have it done."

So I sent the tape to Nashville and I had some records made. I still have the original box, and I've still got about ten of those records… they are on the "Fine" record label. The name on the record is Ronnie Dean. Dean is my middle name, and I ended up having a son named Ronnie Dean, and another named Tyler Dean.

Chapter Seven

Karen

I first met Karen in 1972 when I got out of Vietnam. I came home to Portland and I would go to the Dairy Queen every day. Karen was working up there.

I had this little white German Shepherd puppy that I would take to get ice cream. I'd get some ice cream in a cup, and this little puppy would eat it out of the cup. And Karen was working the counter. I would go there every day. And every day, I'd try to bend over the counter to see her legs, because she had great legs.

I finally asked her out one day, and she said No. I asked her again another day, and she said No. And I asked her a third time, and she finally said Yes.

And the first night we went out, I told her we were going to get married. She said, "You are crazy boy!" We were married three weeks later.

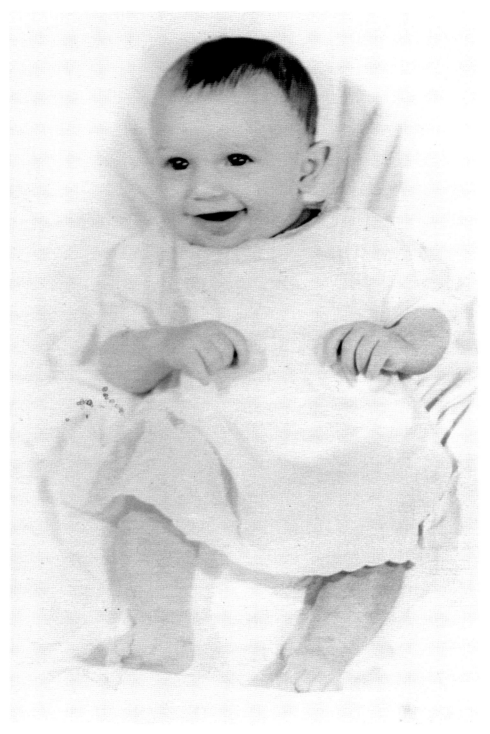

Ronald Dean McDowell. Born March 25, 1950

Ronnie (age 5) with sister Teresa and brother Ricky

McDowell brothers: Denver, Ronnie (age 6), Jerry

7 year old Ronnie

9 years old, with my dad's Ford Fairlane

Having a drink at age 12

8th Grade

16 year old Ronnie McDowell – The real Slim Shady

Most Talented Seniors with Donna Collins. My talent was apparently shoe tying!

When I was 15, I looked like an Ethiopian!

Graduation, Portland High School

Navy, 1968

In the Navy

With my Navy crew. I'm the one on the left with the dark tan

This is the very first time I ever sang on stage. A Navy buddy took the photo

Saying "Hello" to Hong Kong from the deck of the USS Hancock, 1968

RONNIE McDOWELL

My first professional publicity shot

A recording session at the Portland True Value Hardware store!

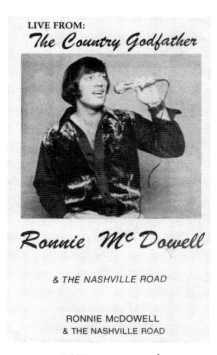

1973 promo card

Another great shot of my band's stylish tuxedo shirts!

*With my daughters Kara and Athena. My brother Ricky and I built the float of the Portland train depot. 1976…
I had no idea what was coming down the tracks a year later*

Signing autographs, 1978

Singing to a packed house at The Old South Jamboree, Walker Louisiana

On my first bus… I bought the bus from Barbara Fairchild

Celebrating my first gold record for 'The King Is Gone'

Riverview Park, Des Moines; July 1978

Signing for fans, 1978

Celebrating a number 1 song with Buddy Killen

On the road again. Front Row: Jackie Brazzel, Jack Hunter, Bill Huntsman Back Row: Ronnie, Ronnie Thurman (Tugboat), Reggie Jaggers, Bo Sloan, Doug Anderson

Wearing my 'aluminum foil' pants! 'Reynolds Wrap' should have sponsored my tour!

The Country Clark Gable

Wichita Falls Texas, May 1980. Courtesy Vicky Houston

Maquoketa Illinois, August 1980. Courtesy Sherry Harkin

A self-portrait I drew in 1980

My Mick Jagger look

Sunny Oak Farm, August 1981. Courtesy Sherry Harkin

On the Grand Ole Opry

Buddy Killen, Mike Curb, Jim Ritz, Ronnie. All three of these men helped me in so many ways. Courtesy Alan Mayor

Tight red leather pants with matching V-neck sweater…and mustache! What was I thinking?!

Muncie Indiana, August 1985. Courtesy Sherry Harkin

Playing for Sam Walton… on the day I lost a million dollars

Ronnie with Buddy Killen

With my friend Conway Twitty

With The Kentucky Headhunters. Fred Young, Richard Young, Ronnie, Greg Martin, Doug Phelps, Ricky Lee Phelps

We meet the King of Bluegrass! Bruce Hunter, Steve Sheperd, Doug Phelps, Bill Monroe, Martin Kicklighter, Ronnie, Greg Martin

On stage with Doug Phelps and Greg Martin. I was going to make fun of Doug's tube socks... until I noticed I didn't have on any pants!

On stage with The Headhunters and my road manager Joe Meador. Courtesy Joe Meador

The night I had the group ACDC as my roadies!

Ronnie and The Killer Jerry Lee Lewis

Ronnie and The Killer Jerry Lee Lewis

Jerry Lee Lewis wears his fur coat as I wear my camo

The Jordanaires along with Millie Kirkham and D.J. Fontana.
Courtesy Dennis Carney Photo Imaging

I loved Millie Kirkham! Courtesy Mike Payne

With the Jordanaires Ray Walker. Ray always does anything he can to make me laugh on stage. Courtesy Mike Payne

Chapter Eight

Beaten By A Ballerina

When I wasn't eating ice cream at the Dairy Queen, I was painting signs. That was my job in the day, and at night I was singing. I formed a band with my little brother Ricky. Our band reminded me of The Blues Brothers. We only knew about seven songs, and we would play them over and over.

We entered a talent contest in Hendersonville, Tennessee. We won the contest, and then we advanced on to a bigger contest in Ashland City. When we won there, we advanced to the finals. They were held in Memphis at the Memphis Coliseum.

We had no doubt we would win it all. We were confident we would bring the top prize home to Portland. But our dreams of the big time came to an abrupt halt when we were beaten by a ballerina! Boy, you talk about putting you in your place and bringing your ego down. All the way home we were shaking our heads, as we kept saying, "A ballerina beat us."

Chapter Nine

Songwriting, Singing… and Scorpions

My brother Ricky was the most talented guy I have ever met. He was born without a thumb. But he could play a guitar and bass without a thumb. He was like a child prodigy. As soon as I got out of the service, we started a band. And he played in my band for a decade.

In the early 70s, Ricky and I started writing songs. And after we wrote quite a few, I started going back and forth to Nashville. I would knock on doors and ask the record companies to listen to my songs. They had an open door policy back then. That's long gone now.

I still have some of the first songs I wrote, and they are pretty bad. But as I learned the songwriting process through the years, I feel like I've gotten better. I do most of my songwriting when I'm driving down the road.

In the mid 70s, Roy Drusky was the first person to ever record one of the songs I had written. I was driving in my car, listening to the Friday Night Frolic on The Grand Ole Opry. And I heard this piano riff, and I said "I know that music". And Roy Drusky, unbeknownst to me, had recorded a song that I'd written called "Deep in the Heart of Dixie". Dixie was a girl. He started singing my song on the Grand Ole Opry, and I literally pulled off to the side of the road. It really shook my whole world. I got out of the car and did a dance around the whole car. I couldn't believe I was hearing Roy Drusky, who I loved, singing one of my songs. That was one of the biggest thrills I ever had.

I went on to have songs recorded by Porter Wagner, Billy Walker, Jean Sheppard, The Wilborn Brothers, and later even George Strait recorded a song I co-wrote.

I love writing songs. I love seeing a song come to life. Writing a song is kind of like raising a kid. You start with a foundation, and then keep adding the layers. You add the guitars and the vocals, and it grows into something very special.

I worked in the local clubs from 1972 to 1977. Five shows a night, six days a week for five years. I painted signs in the day, and was singing in the clubs at night. But even though I was working day and night, we still could not pay our bills. We had no phone. And they were constantly turning our lights and electricity off.

In the spring of 1977, I officially began my recording career when I signed with Scorpion records. Scorpion... known for its venomous stinger... I should have considered it a sign.

The first song I released was "Only The Lonely". Why on earth I did that song, I will never know. I just copied Roy Orbison's version. Of course Roy's was a classic. But no one heard mine. "Only The Lonely" by Ronnie McDowell failed to hit the charts.

With that poor start, no one could have even dreamed that, just a few months later, Ronnie McDowell would be the hottest star in country music.

CHAPTER TEN

THE KING IS GONE

I was the biggest Elvis fan in the world. Still am.

Even today, you can go into any second grade class in America and hold up a picture of George Bush, and they won't have a clue who it is. But if you hold up a picture of Elvis, they know exactly who it is. Explain that to me.

August 16th, 1977, I was driving down the highway. I had the radio on. And the D.J. said Elvis had died. I thought it was a joke, or they were wrong. But I kept turning the radio dial and, sure enough, every station started playing Elvis music.

As I drove, these words started coming into my mind: "I was barely six years old when I first heard him sing…" And I kept writing that song in my head, as I drove from Nashville to Bowling Green, Kentucky, where I was going to work.

As soon as I got off, my friend Bill Huntsman and I took off to Memphis. Like tens of thousands of other fans from around the country, we wanted to go to Graceland to say goodbye to Elvis.

When I got back to Nashville, a friend of mine, Lee Morgan, said "Ronnie, let's do a tribute to Elvis. Let's write a song." I said, "It's funny you say that… listen to this that I started two days ago." Then I listened to what he had written. I had already written the talking part about me listening to Elvis as I grew up, and he said, "Let's just add that to the front of mine." So we combined out thoughts and went into the studio that night.

While we both played equal roles in writing the song, Lee was really the one who made the most important decision about the song. Lee insisted that I sing it like Elvis. He said, "If you do the talking part in that Elvis voice you have, it will really grab people." I just refused to do it. But Lee wouldn't give up. And he was completely right. He should get the credit for insisting that I do it in the Elvis style.

Bucky Barrett played guitar during the "King Is Gone" recording session. I had never met Bucky before. We worked out the arrangement, and then I stepped in front of the mic. Bucky was on the other side of the studio. He was behind a baffle isolation partition with headphones on.

A few seconds after I started singing, I saw Bucky's head rise up over the partition. I saw that his eyes were bugging out. But I knew he was still playing.

As soon as we finished the song, Bucky came over and said, "Man, when you started in, every hair I have stood completely up. I totally thought it was Elvis singing! Did you see me look over to make sure it was you?" I said, "Yeah, I wondered what you were looking at."

The total cost of the recording session was $2,800. When we were finished, Lee asked, "Ronnie, do you have any money?" I said "I have $42." He said he didn't have any money either. So my wife gave me my checkbook, and I wrote $2,800 worth of hot checks to pay for "The King Is Gone".

I went home and slept with that tape. I felt like I had something special.

The next morning, I sat on the steps of Monument Studios and waited for it to open. Gail Pollock drove up and said, "Ronnie, what are you doing here so early?" I said, "Gail, I have a hit. I couldn't sleep all night, so I just came here and waited for you."

I had 15 acetate records made. I also wrote a hot check for those. By the way, I was in such a hurry, I ran out of the studio while the 15th acetate was being made. Gail Pollock took it home with her and kept it for more than thirty years. Then she gave it to me as a very special gift. I still have it today.

Before the hot checks made it to the bank, I was headed to WENO radio in Madison, Tennessee. I don't know why I chose that radio station to go to.

I walked in and told the secretary that I had just recorded a new song and was hoping they would play it. She told me that they didn't take songs off the street, and everything came in from record companies. I responded with just three words: "It's about Elvis."

She took the acetate, told me to hold on, and I watched through the radio studio glass as she walked in and talked to the DJ who was on the air. He looked at me, and then I watched him put the turntable needle down on the record. After listening just a few seconds, he waved for me to come in the studio.

He said, "Hey, I'm gonna play this on the air."

And this is the God's truth... before it even got a fourth way through, the phone lines just lit up. They just went crazy with people calling in! This was just a little AM station. But they had a huge following.

And word then spread to Channel 5, the Nashville TV Station. They called WENO radio and asked to talk to me. They told me to stay at the station. They were coming to interview me. After I did the TV interview, I headed to the big rock radio station WLAC. And when they played it on that station, it completely jammed their telephone lines. It exploded in Nashville, with every radio station playing it as often as they could.

The true overnight success of "The King Is Gone" is hard to explain. It just came from the masses of people from all over the world who loved Elvis. I had nobody to help me promote the song. I had no manager. I did everything on my own. The record just exploded all on its own. That is the simple beauty of it.

"The King is Gone" sold a million records in a week.

How fast did the song hit? I was invited to play the Grand Ole Opry just the night after I recorded the song. Before I went on, Jim Ed Brown put his arm around me and said, "Son, you'll do fine". I said, "Mr. Brown, I'm not scared to go out there. But I just wrote this song two days ago. I don't even know the song." Jim Ed said, "Yeah, I think I would be scared too. Good luck!"

Despite my worries, I went out and nailed the song. I didn't miss a word. And the response I got from the crowd was unbelievable. The crowd went crazy!

Believe it or not, the second I walked off the Opry stage, I got into a car and drove to Chattanooga Tennessee. On the same night that I played the Opry in Nashville, just a couple hours later, I was doing a concert at The Hitchin' Post Club in Chattanooga! And as soon as I walked on stage, the entire crowd rushed the stage. I ran and got behind my drummer. He yelled, "Get away from me! They'll kill me too!" You just had to have been there to see how wild it was.

Not long after "The King is Gone" hit radio, I was on American Bandstand with Dick Clark. I was petrified just to be there. Remember, a few weeks earlier I was working in a club in Bowling Green, Kentucky, making $180 a week, and now I'm on American Bandstand!

Before the show, Dick Clark came by and asked how I was doing. I said, "I'm OK, Mr. Clark. I'm just glad you folks pantomime (lip sync) your songs." Dick said, "Oh, we stopped lip syncing. You've got to sing it live."

Now when I look at that clip of me on Bandstand, it looks like I was in total control. But I was actually scared to death.

That appearance also led to my first meeting with an Elvis impersonator. Before Elvis died, there were only a few "tribute artists". But as I got ready to sing on American Bandstand, I was sitting in the makeup chair and there was a guy dressed like Elvis next to me. His name was Alan. Just one name. He looked over at me and said, in that Elvis voice, "Where you from, boy?" He didn't look like Elvis, but he had a great Elvis voice. He really sang his butt off. That was the first of thousands of meetings I would have over the years with Elvis impersonators.

"The King is Gone" ended up selling over 6 million records. It was so huge that people wanted to know everything about me. That was really a neat time. It was kind of surreal. All of that Elvis energy was being directed toward me.

Some in the business call the time that stardom hits "riding the rocket ship". And that's exactly what I was doing. I was on the ride of my life, going as fast as the rocket ship would take me. I was so busy. There were times when I would have a show in the afternoon in one town, and then we would hit the road, and that night we would do another concert in a different town.

At that time, my mom was working at the Pure Truck Stop on the edge of Portland. There's nothing there now but a concrete slab, but every time I go by there, I think of my friend Rex Graves. In the 50s, he and I would go up there and we'd get barbecue and cornbread, and the cornbread was so big. It cost 35 cents. We loved that barbecue and cornbread!

My mom was working at the truck stop just after "The King is Gone" hit. She was mopping the floor when I ran in. I yelled, "Take that apron off. I have the hottest song in the country and you will never have to work again."

That was the only thing I wanted to do. I wanted to make sure my mother would never have to work again. Helping my mom... that was the highlight of that entire crazy and exciting time.

I am so thankful that both my parents were able to enjoy much of my success. Even though they were divorced, my mom and dad were my biggest fans. They would come to all my shows, and they would be the ones leading the standing ovations. From the stage, I could see my dad standing and clapping, and he was always looking around, making sure everyone else was standing and cheering.

Today, I miss my mother and father so much. One of Vern Gosdin's big hits was "Chiseled in Stone". It has the line, "You don't know lonely...'til it's chiseled in stone". And that is the truth. You never know what lonely feels like until you see the names of your parents chiseled on their tombstone. I wish I could pick up the phone and call them. I'd love to let them know what I am doing, or ask their advice. I miss them every day.

Chapter Eleven

Fame... But Not Much Fortune

The mega success of "The King is Gone" was kind of a blessing and a curse. Everyone thought I was an Elvis impersonator. I didn't wear a white jumpsuit, but I sounded like him. And even today, I still get "You're the guy who does Elvis."

After "The King is Gone" I released quite a few songs, with not very much success. Radio was kind of resisting me. But the fans were going crazy at all of our concerts, whether I had another hit to sing or not.

I had one Top 5 song during that time: "I Love You, I Love You, I Love You" was a huge hit. It was a big country hit, and it was also a pop hit.

I happened to be over in the Carolinas, and there was a guy on the show with me. His name was Bobby Borchers. He was a country singer and songwriter. When he got back to Nashville, he went to Rick Blackburn at Epic Records and said, "This Ronnie McDowell kid... you need to look into signing him. Because the women at his shows were actually tearing his clothes off." And they were.

A short time after that, I was in a recording session at The Sound Shop, which was owned by Buddy Killen. Cliff Williamson was producing me. While I was recording, Buddy happened to walk through. And he told Cliff, "Cliff, you need to let me work with Ronnie." And he ended up working with me for twenty years. Buddy believed in me as a singer and songwriter and, more than that, we became lifelong friends.

When Rick Blackburn heard that Buddy was producing me, he called to ask me to come to Epic. The day I signed my new contract, they gave me a $75,000 signing bonus. Slim Williamson, who owned the Scorpion record company, was there, and I had to hand my entire bonus check over to Slim. Slim said it was for promotion and studio costs. I sold 6 million records for this tiny label, and this was the thanks I got! I learned at that moment that I had been a young kid from Portland, Tennessee. I didn't know anything about lawyers. I had just wanted a hit record. I didn't know anything about the business side of the music business. Boy, I wish I could go back.

For a song that sold millions and millions of records… I only got one check. It was for $26,000. That's all I ever received.

I wish I had been smart. But I wasn't. I was dumber than a bucket of worms.

But I'm not the only story like that. The industry abounds with stories like that. I was just one victim.

Chapter Twelve

Life... And Death

August of 1977 was a life-changing month for me. And the following August would bring another life change.

My son Ronnie Dean was born on August 21, 1978.

But remember how I was born with Alpha 1 antitrypsin deficiency? I ended up giving that same thing to my son. When he was just a few days old, he was at Vanderbilt Hospital. He had tubes connected all over. He had needles in him. The doctors said, "His liver is not producing green bile. We need to punch his liver." That's where they take a huge needle and stick in it your liver, and you almost always die right then. I told them, "No way. I will not let you punch his liver, and I also want you to take all those tubes and needles off of him right now. If he is going to die, he will die at home."

One of the doctors said, "Mr. McDowell, you do have two other children, don't you?" Meaning I would be OK if I lost this boy. I came so close to decking that doctor right there. I took my son and we went home. As soon as we got home, I took his diaper off, and there was green bile in the diaper. I knew he was going live.

My friend Eddie Rabbitt had the same antitrypsin disease I had... and Eddie's son also got it, and he died from it. But the difference between me and Eddie was he was a heavy smoker. I would go up on his bus and he would have an oxygen mask, and he'd breathe in a few breaths of oxygen, and then he'd smoke a cigarette at the same time. He died at the age of 56. The doctors at Vanderbilt told me I would have died in my 40s if I had been a smoker.

Smoking is my very biggest pet peeve. I hate it. My mother died from it. She died from secondhand smoke. She was always with her sister, and her sister always smoked like a chimney.

Cigarettes also killed my little brother Ricky. Ricky was so talented, and he was so funny. But my little brother smoked himself to death. He was the worst smoker I have ever seen.

Ricky always called me "Ranny". One night, I was lying in bed. I was sound asleep. But I was jolted awake when I thought I saw Ricky running at me yelling, "Ranny!" The moment I woke up, the phone rang. It was my cousin JoAnn, and she said, "Ricky is dead."

Chapter Thirteen

The Voice Of Elvis

In 1978, Record World Magazine named me their Most Promising Male Artist. Mel McDaniel was ranked at #2. John Conlee came in at #4.

While I was thrilled to receive that honor, I was having trouble finding a follow up hit to "The King is Gone".

But even without another Top Ten, I had no trouble filling up concert halls. It seemed that everywhere I played, the crowds kept getting bigger and bigger.

And I became a better performer with each show in front of those huge crowds.

I love to entertain. I love to involve the audience in what I'm doing. I like to make them laugh. I want the audience to have a good time.

Al Jolson was the first performer to actually get down in the audience. He would get off the stage and go into the crowd. Before him, especially in Shakespeare's time, it was thought that the performer should be above the audience, and not touch them. But I found that if I adopted Jolson's attitude, that I would become a better entertainer. I know my fans, and my audience likes it when I step off the stage and come meet them in the crowd. Some of the best parts of my show happen during those moments when I'm in the crowd. You never know what will happen.

I am proud to say that I have performed in every state in the U.S. Before one of those concerts, I received a call backstage. The person who answered the phone told me that Dick Clark was holding for me. A couple years had now passed since my very successful appearance on Dick's American Bandstand.

Dick was calling to offer me the chance to do all of the Elvis vocals in a new movie he was producing. He told me Priscilla Presley was helping with the movie that would star Kurt Russell as Elvis. I stood there, holding the phone thinking, "Kurt Russell is that kid from the Disney movies. He doesn't look anything like Elvis."

How wrong I was! Kurt Russell won an Emmy for his role. He blew me away with his performance.

But I didn't want to do the movie. I was already stereotyped with the Elvis stuff. I was still trying to establish myself as Ronnie McDowell. But Dick insisted, saying "Ronnie, we've listened to everyone, and we don't want anyone but you."

I ended up singing 43 songs in the movie. We recorded them in just two days. I was very proud to be a part of the entire project, and it led to many more Elvis-related things.

Over the years I have done the voice of Elvis in 12 movies, 29 commercials, and a Twilight Zone episode. But none of those opportunities would have come my way, were it not for a small kindness I did for a dear friend.

While Dick Clark was impressed with me when I was on American Bandstand, something else led him to offer me the part in the Elvis movie. On my "The King is Gone" album, we included just one Elvis song. I didn't even want to do that. But the great Mae Axton, who wrote "Heartbreak Hotel" for Elvis, asked me to put it on the album. I did not want to get known as an Elvis impersonator, so I was very reluctant. But Mae was such a sweet woman. So, as a favor to her, I put it on the album.

When they were looking for someone to sing the Elvis songs in the movie, Jim Ritz, who was a producer and actor on the show "Happy Days", told Dick Clark, "I have this album that you need to hear. Ronnie McDowell does "Heartbreak Hotel" and he is dead on. You cannot tell that it is not Elvis."

It is kind of like the message in the movie "It's A Wonderful Life": every life touches so many others. If I had not done that kindness to my friend Mae Axton and put her song on my album, Jim Ritz would never have heard me. If Jim had not passed the word on to Dick Clark, I would never have been chosen for the movie. And that movie led to so much more in my career. It led to me meeting and working with all of Elvis' family and friends and band members. It led to so many other projects and, more importantly, to so many other friendships and relationships I have had.

I have no idea what path my life would have taken, if I had not included "Heartbreak Hotel" on that first record.

In the early 80s, Mae Axton said these words to me when we were shooting a video... she said, "Ronnie, you are a very special man. I mean that from the depth of my heart. As I used to tell Elvis, I am so glad that God let me walk the same highway that you have walked."

I treasure that video. And I treasure my friendship with Mae. What a lovely person.

Here are a few more thoughts about the making of the '"Elvis" movie...

When Jim Ritz played my version of "The Wonder of You" for Priscilla Presley, she just could not believe it was not Elvis!

The movie was so popular that Dick Clark made a deal to show it in theaters in Japan and Europe. But they asked that they put in more Elvis music. So they brought back the entire cast, including Kurt Russell, and they filmed more music scenes. They expanded the concert scene at the end of the film, and turned it into a real mini-concert with a number of songs. I recorded those songs in Nashville, and Kurt Russell lip-synched again to my voice in Hollywood.

Now, when you buy the DVD version of the movie, they include that mini-concert at the end.

Many people are shocked to find out that I never met Kurt Russell during the filming of '"Elvis"! And I have still never met Kurt Russell. It almost happened a couple times, but I still have not met him.

They aired the 3-hour "Elvis" movie during Sweeps week. That's the most important ratings period of the year. Back then, there were only three major TV networks. That night, our '"Elvis" movie was on ABC. NBC had "Gone With the Wind", and CBS aired "One Flew Over The Cuckoo's Nest". And we beat both of those! That shows you the power of Elvis.

One of my all-time favorite actors was, and still is, Clark Gable. And we beat "Gone With the Wind"!

I can picture ol' Clark's reaction: "Frankly Ronnie, I don't give a damn!"

Chapter Fourteen

We Want Elvis!
But Does Anyone Want Ronnie?

I get asked many times, what is my favorite Elvis song to sing. I have two favorites. They are "Don't Be Cruel" and "It's Now Or Never".

There are a couple songs that are very hard to sing. I performed with the Memphis Symphony for Elvis' 60th birthday, and I had to do "If I Can Dream", and that is a tough song to sing. "Jailhouse Rock" is another hard song to sing. It was hard for Elvis when he recorded it. He did half the song, then took a break to eat lunch, and then went back to do the other half. It is a tough song.

But at this point in my career, I found that I was having a tough time singing just about any Elvis song. And after the huge success of the Kurt Russell movie, I once again found myself trying to break out of the Elvis stereotype. Many nights, I would get discouraged when I would be on stage singing my own songs and some drunk would yell out, "Do 'Love Me Tender!'" And even today, some people still don't care about "Older Women" or all the other hits I've had. They remember me doing Elvis. But that is something you live with, and that's OK.

I started my recording career with Scorpion Records. Then I was with Epic for seven years. Then I met Mike Curb, and I've been at Curb Records ever since.

Chart success was hard to come by for me in the 1970s. But all of my hard work would soon pay off, as I found out that the 1980s would be MY decade!

The decade started with a bang as I just missed the very top of the charts. We hit number two with "Wandering Eyes", and we followed that up with my first number one song, "Older Women"!

"Older Women" was produced by Buddy Killen. Buddy produced all of Exile's number one records. He also worked with Roger Miller, Joe Tex, and so many others. Buddy and I had a lot of success together, with a lot of big hit records.

The Jordanaires were on that session. They were also there for "Wandering Eyes" and for "I Love, I Love You". I had fought to have everyone, all of the musicians and singers all together in the studio. I didn't want to be separated in a booth. I really had to fight for that. We did one take of the song, and Buddy Killen jumped out of his chair, raised his arms and said, "What else do we need to do? That's perfect!" One take. We put that song out and it went straight to number one!

Chapter Fifteen

News Flash: Billy Graham Loves Older Women!

I did a show in Winston, Salem with Conway Twitty. We were at the Holiday Inn. I was going up to my room when the elevator doors opened up, and there stood the Reverend Billy Graham and his wife. I said "Mr. Graham, it is an honor to meet you." He said, "Who are you, young man?" I said, "I'm Ronnie McDowell. I sing Country Music. I'm here in concert tonight with Conway Twitty. " And I never will forget, he said, "Oh, yes, you are the one who has that "Older Women". Me and my wife love that song!"

Chapter Sixteen

Conway

This might take awhile.

I could write an entire book just about my friendship with Conway Twitty.

I went on tour with Miss Teenage America... her stage name was Jessica James, but her real name was Kathy Twitty. She was Conway's daughter. She and I hit it off. I told her I would give anything to meet her dad. She told me to come to his office that next week. I was so thrilled.

Back in the 1970s, one of the big status things to show that you were really successful, was how thick your carpet was. That old shag carpet. And when I walked into Conway's office, it was covered with white carpet, and I swear it seemed like it was ten inches tall. And every step I took, I seemed to make tracks in that thick carpet. It was like snow.

Conway was sitting behind the desk, and he was so great looking. He was slim and tanned, and he looked like a million bucks. And he stuck his hand out and said, "Son, how would you like to open my shows?" I said, "Twist my arm!"

I worked with Conway on the road for six years. I did many concerts with Conway and Loretta Lynn. We did tours that featured me, Randy Travis, Conway and Loretta. They named the tour "The Country Music Explosion". That was one of the great things about Conway... whoever was hot at the time, it didn't matter if it was Randy Travis or George Strait, he would add them to his show. Can you imagine, on one stage... Conway, Loretta, George Strait, and me. I was just thrilled to be there.

Not only did I start opening his shows, but I signed on with his booking agency United Talent.

The moment I met Conway Twitty, I saw his spirit. He was one of the greatest guys ever on the planet Earth.

I talked to Conway about everything.

I also spent more than three decades in Conway's bus!

I had originally bought Barbara Fairchild's bus. I used the money I got from "The King is Gone", the $26,000... most of that money went to the down payment for that bus. The total cost was $67,000. But it was an older bus.

I was opening shows for Conway. I was also on Conway's softball team. We were playing ball and Conway said, "You need to get rid of that old bus and you need to buy mine." He said, "I've only had it two years and it ain't got that many miles on it. It's only got 2 million miles on it." I said, "2 million miles!"

But Conway talked me into it. I sold my old one to the Bellamy Brothers and I bought Conway's bus. And I ended up putting another 5 million miles on it. So that bus has more than 7 million miles! I traveled in that bus for thirty years.

I loved to play jokes on Conway. Once, I was at a truck stop and I found one of those little boxes that would laugh when you turned it one way, and when you turned it the other way it would laugh again. We were in Branson. Conway was on stage and he was singing "The Clown". It was a serious song, but there was a line about a clown. While he was singing, he had his eyes closed, and he was really into it. And when he got to the line, "Our love is like a circus baby and I'm just the clown...", I had a microphone just behind the curtain, and I put that box up to the mic and it started laughing. Conway jumped back and yelled, "You son of a bitch, you scared the hell out of me!" Right there into the microphone on stage! And everyone in that place just lost it.

Everybody thought he was going to kill me. But when the show was over, he came off stage. He was laughing and said, "You got me!"

I was always aggravating him, constantly. He would start his show off each night with his classic "It's Only Make Believe". He would sing the line, "People see us everywhere". But every now and then, when he didn't expect it, they would leave his mic off, and I would be backstage, and I would sing the line instead. He would freak out. He said, "What the hell is goin' on?!"

It broke the monotony of traveling, of doing one date after another, and moving on to the next city night after night. We would do things to cut up and have fun.

He was the biggest star in the world. Conway was so huge at that time. I was just glad to be there on the show.

Staunton, Virginia is where all my folks are from. The McDowell cemetery is just outside Staunton. Near there, on Highway 81 going up to Washington, there is a White's Truckstop. We always stopped there, because Conway loved their Chip Beef and Gravy on bread. Conway said, "This is the best stuff I have ever ate in my life."

He was my mentor. But he would get on to me. He would tell it like it is. He would sometimes talk to you like he was a school principal, or like he was your dad. And he really was like my second dad. That's the God's truth. If he felt like saying something to you, he didn't care if it hurt your feelings or not, he would tell you. Sometimes I wish I could be that way, that forthcoming and honest.

One day he asked me, "Where did you get that song 'You're Gonna Ruin My Bad Reputation?'" I said, "A young guy named Jeff Crossan wrote it. It's the first song he's ever had recorded." Conway said, "Do not get any more songs from him. That is the worst song I have ever heard in my life!"

Two weeks later, the song was #1. Conway called me and said, "Well McDougal..." (that's what he called me, McDougal), "if you can take that song to number one, you are a hell of a lot better than I thought you were."

He was always on me about my show. He said "You are not a comedian! You don't need to tell jokes. And you don't need to be out there moving all around. All you need to do is stand there and sing 'em your songs. That's what they come to hear." That was his philosophy and it worked for him. But I said, "Conway, that's fine for you. You have more than 40 number one songs to sing. You could do four hours of number one songs. I only have two. I have to do other things to entertain the crowd. I have to move around."

On my 29th birthday, he said, "I have a song for you." He had the 45 record, and he was spinning it on his finger. He said, "Listen to it. It will be a number one song if you do it." I listened to it, and I took it back to him and said, "Conway, I don't think it's a hit." He said, "OK, I'll do it." The song was "Happy Birthday Darlin'". It went to #1.

One night in Louisville, Kentucky, we were on the bus and Conway played a song that he thought would be good for me. It was "I'd Love to Lay You Down." I said, "Conway, that is the dirtiest song I have ever heard in my life." He said, "It's about a man and his wife." I said, "I don't care. It is filthy. Who in the world is going to play a song like that? You might as well come right out and say it... 'I'd love to lay you down'... I can't do it." Conway did it. It turned out to be a huge, number one hit. It was one of his all-time biggest hits.

I once asked Conway why he offered me the first chance to record the great songs he had found. I asked "Why do you give them to me first?" He said, "Because I believe in you Ronnie." That's all the accolades I need. I need no other accolade from the music industry. When Conway Twitty said, "I believe in you", that was more than enough for me. Nobody believed in me like he did.

Many fans thought Conway was stuck up. But he was shy. I am very shy. But Conway was ten times worse than me. While I kind of grew out of my shyness, he never did.

In 1980, we did "It's Only Make Believe" together. We sped it up from the original version Conway did. He originally didn't want to be on the record. He said it could be a hit without him. But I talked him into it.

The last time I talked to Conway, we were in Branson. I had just recorded an album of classic old songs. It was called "For Your Precious Love." I was walking across the parking lot of Roy Clark's theater, and Conway was sitting there in his Pacer. He called me over and said, "Do you hear what I'm listening to?" He was listening to my new album. He said, "I love this. But you are not going to get it played on the radio. They are looking for excuses to not play me and you anymore." I said, "Conway, they are not going to stop playing you." He said, "No, they are trying to come up with a reason to take me off of radio." I could see that really hurt him.

I knew how it felt when radio quit playing my songs. The rude and awful things they were saying to me. I couldn't understand why. I hadn't done anything. I had done everything I was supposed to do. I was nice to program directors. I called them to thank 'em for playing my records. I know how it devastated me. Some performers turn to alcohol and drugs when that happens. But I did not. My priorities were right. My priorities were with my children. I knew that I had to stay strong and focused, for them. But some people need that applause. I saw the stress on Conway. It was killing him. Can you imagine if you have 50 number one records, and all of the sudden the industry that had helped you all those years just starts to turn its back on you for no reason?

They say stress settles in your gut. That's where that aneurysm busted in his stomach, and I will always believe that stress caused his veins and arteries to weaken.

Conway had just finished a show in Branson, and they had started home to Nashville. Conway asked his bus driver, Billy Parks, "What was it like when you passed your kidney stone?" That's what he thought it was. He went in the bathroom of the bus and fell down.

When they got to the hospital in Springfield, the doctor told him, "Conway, you have an aneurysm that we have to go in and fix." And Conway's last words were "Well, if that's what you got to do, let's do it."

I will never forget how I learned that Conway had died.

I was in Mrytle Beach, South Carolina. I left the hotel that morning and got on the bus that Conway sold me. As soon as we got on the highway, we turned the radio on and they were in the middle of my duet with Conway, "It's Only Make Believe." And I thought, "that's cool that they are playing our song". But at the end of it, the DJ said, "That's the late, great Conway Twitty." And that's how I found out my friend was gone.

Chapter Seventeen

How To Lose A Million Dollars... Twice

In the early 1980s, I was hired by the Walmart Corporation to do a show for their employees in Bentonville, Arkansas.

Before the show, me and my son Ronnie Dean were playing catch in the Walmart parking lot. Ronnie missed the ball, and it hit him in the face. He fell down and started crying. And this old man who was in an old pickup truck came running out, and he actually got to Ronnie before I did.

As we talked, I told him I was playing for the Walmart folks. The old man said, "I'm the one who hired you. I'm Sam Walton."

We talked for about a half hour, and he asked me how much money I had when I got out of the Navy. I said I had $700. He told me, "If you had invested that $700 in my Walmart stock, that $700 be worth more than a million dollars!" But of course I didn't.

If I would have been smart, I should have told him, "Mr. Walton, just take my pay for tonight's show and put it into stock for your company right now." Of course, once again, I didn't. This was the early 80s, and who knows how much that Walmart stock would be worth today!

Chapter Eighteen

THE HEADHUNTERS

In 1981, when I was on the road with Conway, I decided I needed a band with an edgier sound. So I started adding new members to my group. A decade later, those new members would be known as The Kentucky Headhunters.

When I called Doug Phelps, he was in college. Believe it or not, Doug was actually going to college to be a coach. He had planned to be a high school basketball and baseball coach. He was 20 years old. He had a natural talent for both sports and music. When I offered him the job, he dropped out of college.

Greg Martin had been in a band with Richard and Fred Young. Greg had more of a rock background, and was into rock music, but I invited him to Portland to audition. He played three or four songs, and I asked him if he would happen to be available to play with me on the TV show "Hee Haw" the next day.

Doug and Greg were real edgy pickers. And I just felt they were right for me. Everyone thought I was crazy when I got these long-haired boys. But they fit like a glove. They were country boys like I was. They were cut from the same cloth as I am. We all came up the hard way. They were great artists and musicians. But they were better friends.

Eventually, Richard Young joined us to play rhythm guitar and sell my concessions. Ricky Phelps came out to sing and play guitar. And Fred Young even came out and played drums with me some. So at one point, I had all of The Kentucky Headhunters in my band. But Doug and Greg were with me for eight years. And they started writing "Dumas Walker" on Conway's bus.

I knew they were talented. That's why I hired them. And I would let them show their talent on stage. Doug Phelps is one of the best players I have ever heard. Greg Martin is one of the great guitar players of our time. He slept with his guitar. I'm not kidding. He actually slept with his guitar!

My song "It's Only Make Believe"… that's the Kentucky Headhunters singing on it. Me and Conway and the Headhunters. They did all the harmonies and all the pickin'.

My "I'm Still Missing You" album was a real innovative and edgy album for me. It was the Headhunters' influence on that album.

The Headhunters worked with me from October 1981 to mid 1989. Greg and Doug probably worked more dates with me than they have done as The Headhunters, even after all these years.

Greg and Doug say they went to "Ronnie McDowell University." All of the TV shows we did, along with all the video shoots, recording sessions and thousands of concerts, helped prepare them for all the things they would be thrown into when they became The Kentucky Headhunters.

When they were trying to land a record deal, the group had a showcase for all the record company officials and all the powerful music people in Nashville. But just before what would be the most important concert of their lives, they had been out on tour with me the night before, and they were almost late to their own showcase! They were so late, they had to change clothes in the parking lot; then they threw their instruments up on stage and just took off. They didn't even have time for a sound check.

And the performance they gave that night sent them into the big time. Harold Shedd, the head of Mercury Records, was blown away by the group, and he signed them to his label.

Even though they had the backing of a major record company, when they left my group, I know they were worried if they were doing the right thing. I know Greg was torn about leaving. So I told them that I would hire them back if things didn't work out.

But I knew they would do great. But none of us had any idea they would skyrocket to the top as fast as they did.

A short time later, The Headhunters recorded their landmark album "Pickin' On Nashville" at the Soundshop where I recorded my stuff.

I have always been so proud of all of those guys. I will always be proud of them. And I am proud that I had a hand in putting them all together.

CHAPTER NINETEEN

Mom Always Said To Wear Clean Underwear In Case...
(A few of my most memorable road experiences)

One of the craziest things that happened to me was in Scottsboro, Alabama. It was when that Elvis emotion was so high. Back then, I didn't wear any underwear. I don't know why, but for some reason I didn't wear underwear. That was a mistake.

When I walked on stage, those women grabbed my ankles and pulled me down. And all the girls just rushed the stage. I had a hold of my pants, trying to keep them up. My bus driver ran out on stage and grabbed me under the shoulders. I was trying to pull my pants up, and the women were trying to pull them off. But luckily, they weren't able to get them off. That would have been so embarrassing. Can you imagine?!

One night, we were in Columbus, Ohio. And the concert hall had a big orchestra pit. The audience couldn't see down in the pit, but we could see into it from the stage.

I was in the middle of a song. Conway Twitty's drummer was named Pork Chop. He was a great guy, but he was a big, overweight guy. I was on stage in the middle of the show, and I looked down, and our bus driver had Pork Chop in a wheelbarrow and Pork Chop was buck naked! Our driver was pushing him around the orchestra pit! I lost it. I started laughing so hard and the fans had no idea what I was laughing about. And they just kept pushing him around. That was a sight you would never want to see, and I don't want to see anything like that again.

There was an artist who was starting to become a big star, and today he is a huge star. He was on the road with me and Conway. We were in a Holiday Inn, and he had gotten drunk on Jack Daniels, and someone put him in a wheelbarrow. He didn't have any clothes on and they were pushing him down the hallway of the hotel!

I don't know what it is about country stars having to get naked when they see a wheelbarrow! I have no idea where they even found those wheelbarrows.

I have so many stories about Jerry Lee Lewis. But one of my favorite memories is of the first time I ever met him.

I was on a bus with Jerry Lee and Hank Williams, Jr. You can imagine how that was. I was on a show with both of them in Millington, Tennessee.

"The King is Gone" was the biggest record in the world, and they threw me on a show with all of my heroes. And I loved Hank, Jr.

I went to the bus and Merle Kilgore, Hank's manager, opened the door. Merle wrote "Ring of Fire" for Johnny Cash, and also the classic "Wolverton Mountain". I told Merle I would like to meet Jerry Lee and Hank. He led me to the back and I knocked on the door. That door flew open and Jerry Lee Lewis jumped right in my face. He put his index finger on my nose and said "Are you a Baptist, boy?" I said, "Yes Sir." He said, "Well them Baptists ain't worth a damn!" Those were the first words Jerry Lee ever said to me!

I didn't have a bus yet. I was traveling in a car while my band was in another vehicle. I was in a big yellow Continental. We called it the canary.

We went to Gallatin, Tennessee and bought a new van and trailer. We thought we were really in the big time!

Our van and trailer were still brand new when I got a call one day.

It was one of my band members. He said, "Ronnie, you are not going to believe this, but that trailer came off the van. It rolled off the road and right into a creek. All of our instruments are floating down the creek right now."

Welcome to the big time!

The biggest show I ever did was in Detroit, Michigan. It was me and The Oak Ridge Boys, and a bunch of others. There were 60,000 people in the stadium. I was in the middle of singing, and I could see this girl running up toward the stage. She was in a dead run, and I could tell she wasn't stopping. She leaped on the stage and grabbed me. There were four policemen trying to get her off of me. It was a little scary for a few moments. But sometimes fans can get pretty excited.

I remember another show in Detroit for a different reason.

Me and Conway had a concert there, and our opening act was a little fourteen year old girl. But she blew everyone away with her amazing voice. Her name was Celine Dion.

Let that be a lesson… that you always need to be nice to your opening act… they might end up owning Las Vegas!

Randy Travis got sick and couldn't do a show, so they called me to fill in at the last minute. My friend Larry Collins loaned us his small jet. And we didn't realize, after we loaded the band and all of our gear and equipment, that we had overloaded the plane. When we took off, we just barely cleared the little Portland runway. We could have easily crashed and killed everyone. I like traveling by bus much more than flying.

I loved having the legendary Scotty Moore come out on tour with us.

Of course, Scotty was with Elvis when they started at Sun Records. It was Elvis, Scotty and Bill Black. A short time later, D.J. Fontana started playing drums for them. And those four changed the world of music forever.

When we traveled, Scotty loved to drink that Johnnie Walker Red Whiskey. And he would drink so much that he would pass out. He would be completely passed out, even though he was still sitting up in his chair on the bus. One night when he was passed out, we covered him with fruit. We put grapes, bananas, cherries and apples all over him!

When he woke up, we showed him the pictures we had taken. Scotty looked at the photos and said, "Ronnie, bend over and I'll show you my banana!"

I always liked to try to distract Scotty Moore when he was in the middle of a guitar solo. He was such a professional that you could do almost anything and he would not even flinch.

One time, he was playing and I kissed him on the cheek. As he was still playing, he whispered in my ear, "You kiss me one more time and we'll have to get a room!"

We were at the Rum Boogie Cafe on Beale Street in Memphis. I was there with the Kentucky Headhunters.

I saw this really short guy dancing with this super tall woman. Greg Martin, my guitar player, said, "Hey, that's Angus Young." I asked, "Who is that?" Greg said, "He has been with the group AC/DC since 1973." It turned out that AC/DC was in the club. Angus was just over 5 feet tall and he was dancing with a girl who was over 6 foot tall! Greg went over and introduced himself, and they started talking about their love of Chuck Berry.

Then Greg asked him about the tall girl. Angus said, "Yeah, she is pretty tall… but she is worth the climb!"

We visited a while, and then I asked if they'd like to go out and see the town. They said, "Yeah mate. Tonight we will be your roadies!"

They had on shorts, t-shirts and caps. No one knew who they were. No one had a clue that my "roadies" were one of the biggest rock bands in the world.

In 1992, Danny Rasberry booked me with Gene Watson for a concert in Laurel, Mississippi. The crowd was so huge that people were literally hanging from the rafters.

But before the show, I took Scotty Moore and D.J. Fontana to visit a local elementary school. I played a few songs for the students, and we talked about music history. Can you imagine being a 5th grader, and you are music class learning about Elvis when Scotty Moore and D.J. Fontana walk in?!

I asked my friend Jim Calloway to be an opening act for me as a comedian. Jim is also from Portland, Tennessee. He is as funny as Robin Williams. He could go on Jimmy Fallon tonight and bring down the house.

We played a little bar in Georgia. Everybody was drunk and Jim was telling his jokes, but he couldn't buy a laugh. It was a tough crowd.

But the next night, we moved into a big auditorium in Charlotte. I was backstage, waiting for Jim to finish his act, and I heard the crowd absolutely going nuts. They were laughing so hard, I thought, "Wow, Jim is really killing them." I went to the side of the stage and peaked out behind the curtain, and Jim was standing there wearing a suit coat and tie… and no pants! He had on a huge pair of boxer shorts! And they had big red hearts on them.

He was so skinny, it looked like a pair of boxers on a pencil.

He told the crowd, "Ronnie McDowell told me to give a brief act…"

After the show, he was helping me as I signed autographs. A woman came up to him and said, "Son, you look a lot better with your pants on!"

We were needing a bus driver. And I found us one.

We always left late at night, and we agreed to meet the band at the Lebanon, Tennessee truck stop.

As everyone loaded onto the bus, Marvin Kicklighter, who we all called Rooster, saw this guy walking across the parking lot. The guy had bib overalls on and Rooster said, "Look, here comes Farmer Brown!" I saw him and said, "That's Fred. He's our bus driver. He drove my school bus the entire time I was in school."

Joe Meader, my manager, said, "Ronnie, this is a different world. Just because he could handle a school bus does not mean he can drive us cross country." I said, "Just give him a chance."

But when he walked onto the bus, Fred said, "Good God! Which one is the brake and which one is the gas?!"

So Joe gave him a quick lesson and said, "You watch as Steve, our keyboard player, gets us out of town, and then we'll switch drivers."

We had to be in Dover, Delaware by 2:00 the next afternoon. We knew we had 14 hours to get there. When we got to Crossville, Tennessee, my former school bus driver said, "I think I can take over." He got behind the wheel and he was going about 40 miles an hour. Joe said, "You've got to go faster than that." He answered, "I have never run fast in a bus!"

Joe watched him as long as he could, but he had to get some sleep. So he told him, "At 7 AM, you yell and get me up and I'll take over."

Well, Joe got up at about 6 AM and he saw we were barely moving. He ran up front and Fred had his head laying on the steering wheel. He was totally slumped over! He looked up at Joe and said, "I've never been so tired in all my life."

Joe said, "Well, how far are we?" Fred answered, "Bristol." (Bristol is only about 3 hours from Crossville) Joe screamed, "Bristol, Tennessee?! God a mighty! Pull this thing over as soon as you can!"

I heard the yelling and came up from the back. Joe saw me and said, "Your famous school bus driver has driven all night and we are only to Bristol, Tennessee!"

We pulled into the next rest area. A few sleepy band members jumped out to go to the bathroom, and Joe said he would take over driving.

Joe told us, "Buckle up back there, because we will have to go 90 miles an hour for the next eight hours to get to Dover on time."

Joe had been going about 95 miles an hour for three hours when he got a call over the CB: "Blue Stagecoach, this is the Highway Patrol." Joe put on the brakes, but the trooper said, "Don't worry, I am not behind you. But did you stop at a rest area in Bristol?"

Joe said yes. The trooper radioed, "Ronnie's Uncle Willard got off the bus to go to the bathroom. He is with me and we have been trying to catch you for the last three hours. We have been going almost 100 miles an hour and we haven't caught you yet."

He went on, "Uncle Willard says since you are in a hurry, that you should just go on and you can pick him up in Baltimore tomorrow. I will take him to the next truck stop and help him catch a truck that's headed to Baltimore."

Well, we made it to Dover... 2 hours late. But the show went on.

My school bus driver felt so bad. And after the show he said, "I'm sorry, but this is the first time I've ever been out of Tennessee. When are we going back home?" Joe told him, "We are out for a week straight on this run." Fred said, "Good God, I don't have any clothes except what I've got on!"

He did get better, once he got the hang of it. But that was the only time he went on the road with us.

I would also like to say that Fred Cluggs, my former school bus driver, was a wonderful guy. He was also a great musician. Fred passed away on Christmas Eve of 2014.

I was playing the Coliseum in Alexandria, Louisiana when Doug Phelps, who was in my band, came on the bus. He said, "Hey, you need to come check out this guy who is your opening act. He looks like George Strait, but he's playing Marshall Tucker and Lynyrd Skynyrd." I went out and watched and said, "That's different, alright." My opening act was Garth Brooks.

We did two nights in a row with David Allen Coe. One night was at the Orpheum Theatre in Memphis, and the next night was in Jackson, Tennessee.

That was kind of a unique pairing, since our styles are so different.

David was very nice to all of us. But he got mad at his crew. During his sound check, his battery on his guitar went out, and he smashed his guitar down on the stage and stormed off.

But at show time, he was back and just blew the crowd away.

I was at Opryland playing for a Grocery convention. And before I went on, the guy in charge said, "I want to warn you that when you start, most of the crowd will not pay any attention to you, and some will just get up and walk around." And he was right! As soon as I started, the crowd left! But I told the boys, "Well, they are paying us big bucks, so let's give 'em their money's worth"... and we did our full show to a bunch of empty chairs.

I sang at the Lincoln Center two times. I went there with my producer, Buddy Killen. I took my daughter Kara. She loves all that history in Washington.

On one of those trips, Michael Keaton, who played Batman, was also there. I was singing the National Anthem and I surprised Michael by having him come up and sing a line of the Anthem with me. At the end, he whispered to me "I'm gonna kill you." But he did great.

President George Bush, the first President Bush, was having a rally in Cincinnati, and they asked me to perform. As I was singing, here came this helicopter with the President.

They landed. He got off, walked up on stage, and said to the crowd, "I would like to thank Ronnie McDowell for performing here today."

What an honor it is, when you hear the President of United States say that. I never thought a President would say my name.

For many years, I didn't have a "star suite" in the back of the bus like most artists. I just used a regular bunk like the band did. The beds are stacked on top of each other. I usually slept on the lower bunk, and Greg Martin had the top bunk just above me. If you have ever been in a tour bus, you know there is very little room in between bunks, and they look very similar to a coffin.

One night, Greg woke me up screaming, "Ronnie, you are having a nightmare!" He said I was screaming, "Let me out! Let me out!" I was pushing as hard as I could on the bottom of his bunk.

When he woke me, I said, "I was dreaming that I was in a casket!"

We were in Michigan, working at a casino that was owned by an Indian tribe.

We did a couple nights there. After our shows, we went out and I bought a huge bottle of Crown Royal. I drank just a little before bed. The next morning, we left the hotel. We had driven about 15 minutes when I realized I had left an overnight bag and that big bottle of Crown Royal in my room.

So we turned around and went back. My friend Jim Calloway walked me up to my room, and when we walked in, there were three Indian men... the housekeepers... and they had already drank half of my bottle of Crown Royal! Two of them were sitting on the bed, and the other was sitting on a chair holding the bottle!

I grabbed my overnight bag and just waved at them as I walked out.

Every now and then, you will encounter a fan who will go to any lengths to get to you.

One time, a woman ran right onto the bus. I was in the back and Joe Meador, my road manager, was in the front. He stood up to stop her and she just ran right through him. She knocked him flat on his back, and actually walked right over him, and she was wearing high heel shoes. She was actually going to walk right over his face, and right when her heel got ready to go into Joe's mouth, he grabbed her shoe and took her down.

He was so mad, he opened the bus door and threw her out. He forgot that we were parked on a big hill, and when she hit the ground, she rolled down that hill. Her high heel shoes flew off about halfway down, but she made it all the way to the bottom.

We did a show in Knoxville in 1981.

Lacy J. Dalton opened the show. The group Alabama went on second.

I followed Alabama, and then Tom T. Hall closed the show. He had more hits than all of us combined, but by the time me and Alabama got through with that crowd, everyone was worn out when Tom T. came on.

A short time later, we did a concert in North Carolina. Alan Jackson was the opening act! Then Alabama came on. And then I closed the show.

I could tell that Alabama was getting ready to be huge. You could feel the excitement they brought to the crowd.

But Alan was just a tall, quiet guy. He sang good, but we had no idea that he would go on to become the true superstar that he is. No one had a clue.

In July 2015, Sue Zwires came all the way from Michigan to one of my shows in Gallatin, Tennessee. I was in concert with The Drifters.

But Sue got there late, and the show was almost over.

By the time I found out about it, Sue was already back out to her car. She has to use a wheelchair. I asked The Drifters if they would go outside with me. Sue was sitting in her car, so me and The Drifters just opened all the car doors and sang to Sue and her friends. We sang acapella, with no music, right there in the street under the street lights.

I really try to take care of my fans. What can you say about fans who come all the way from Michigan to Gallatin, Tennessee? We should have done our entire show for them out in the street at their car.

People think country "stars" are loaded, and that they are always walking around with a lot of money. Think again.

I was headed for a show with George Jones in Pigeon Forge, Tennessee. My band had left early from Nashville, and I was going to drive in a car with my friend Allen Coker. Allen sold my t-shirts and other merchandise at my shows.

We had just left town when we saw a sign that said: "Boiled Peanuts." We both thought that sounded good, so we pulled over to get some. But when I went to pay for them, I realized that I didn't have any money on me... not one cent! I looked at Allen and he said, "I only have $3.00." So we asked them to give us $3.00 worth of peanuts.

We got in the car and I said, "I hope these peanuts don't make us thirsty, because we don't have any money to buy a drink!"

We had to drive the rest of the way to Pigeon Forge and we didn't have one dime on us. No one knows what the real life of an entertainer is.

I played Tombstone Junction, Kentucky for years. It was like a small Dollywood. One of my biggest fans, Lucille Frye, came to see me there. Lucille lived in Kentucky, but she would go to every Ronnie McDowell show she could get to. She was one of those truly devoted fans. She thought I hung the moon. She loved me so much.

At Tombstone Junction, they had one of the old time photo places where you dress up and they take a black and white photo. Lucille asked me if I would put on a civil war uniform and pose for a picture with her. There was no way I was going to say No to that woman. So we got into the civil war clothes and took our photos.

And when she got home, she hung that photo on her wall. But a very short time later, Lucille passed way. I am so glad that I took the time to take that photo with her.

Before we move on down the road...I want to say thank you to Ronnie Thurman. We never called him Ronnie. He was known to everyone as 'Tugboat'. Tugboat drove my tour bus for 30 years. I have so many stories of going down all those roads with 'Tuggy' behind the wheel. We always knew he would get us there safe and on time.

Chapter Twenty

Eve Said To Adam...
"Clothes don't make the man."

I love Goodwill stores. When I do a concert in a new town, I always try to visit their Goodwill store.

We were playing a show in Greenville, Tennessee, but when we got into town, I realized I had left my stage clothes in my car back in Hendersonville when I got on the bus.

So we went to the Goodwill store, and I found a black suit and shoes for $12! I played the concert that night in my $12 suit... with no alterations. And I liked it so much that I kept it, and I ended up doing a lot of shows in that $12 suit.

We were doing a show in Albuquerque, New Mexico, and we had to fly to the date. Since I didn't want to take a lot of bags, I thought I would just buy some clothes when we got there.

When we landed, I told my manager Don Dortch that I needed to go clothes shopping, and he said he would go along.

I pulled into a Kmart and Don said, "Don't tell me that are going to Kmart to buy an outfit that you are going to wear onstage tonight?!" I said, "Yes I am. There is nothing wrong with Kmart." Don said, "You must be the only country star who buys his outfits at a place that also has a popcorn machine!"

I was doing the show "Nashville Now" on TNN. I got to the studio very late. I had only about ten minutes before I went on. I was dressed in running shorts and a t-shirt. And I thought I had my show clothes in the bus, but they were not in there.

So I asked my manager Don Dortch if I could have his shirt. He took it off, and I put it on. Then I asked him for his shoes. He took those off.

And I said, "I really hate to ask this, but I need your pants." Don just shook his head and started unzipping. He had to watch me do the show, while he sat in the green room in just his underwear! Now that is a true friend.

We were playing Fitzgerald's Casino in Tunica, Mississippi.

It was almost time to go on, and I realized I had no socks. I had a beautiful black suit, but no socks.

So on our way to the stage, I found a state trooper and asked him, "Would you mind if I borrowed your socks?" He looked at me for a minute, and when he realized I wasn't joking, he sat down and took his socks off and gave them to me.

So I did the concert, and the state trooper stood there in his uniform with no socks. After the show, he was still laughing as he told me to just keep them!

Tunica was also the site of another "wardrobe malfunction"...

I was visiting with my friend Allen Coker, just before our show at the Horseshoe Casino. Allen had on a real nice, light blue t-shirt. I asked him if I could wear it during my concert. I thought his dress t-shirt would look good with my black suit.

So, Allen gave it to me and I put it on. It was just a couple minutes before show time, and I was mixing up a little wine. I was going to put the wine in an empty water bottle and take it on stage. Allen told me not to spill any of the wine on my shirt. And before he could even get the words out of his mouth... I did. I spilled that bright wine all down the front of his shirt.

By then it was almost time to go on, and since I didn't have anything else to wear, I just took the shirt off and put it on backwards. I wore it backwards the entire show!

My guitar player and backup vocalist Doug Phelps was always the last one to go to bed on the bus. And he always did pushups and situps before he went to bed. He always had a good physique, and kept himself in good shape.

One night, Doug was doing his exercises and he only had on his underwear. Bruce, our bus driver, yelled back and asked Doug if he could drive for an hour while he took a nap. It was the middle of the night, and Doug just walked up front and took over driving. He was wearing nothing but his underwear. No shirt, no socks, no shoes.

About an hour later, Doug noticed a cop's blue lights behind us. Usually when the cops stop you, they make you wait while they sit in their car behind you. But Doug pulled over and that policeman was right at the door. Doug had no time to put on pants or anything!

The cop looked at him and asked for his driver's license. Doug told him he would have to go to his bunk to get it. When he came back to the front of the bus, the policeman already had his speeding ticket written! He handed Doug the ticket and didn't even ask him why he was driving with no clothes on!

At a show in South Carolina, I sang about three songs and I noticed the audience was laughing. And they just kept laughing.

And I wasn't telling any jokes. I was singing. And they were laughing.

Finally, in between songs, I went to the edge of the stage and asked, "What in the world are you all laughing at?"

I got my answer when the entire front row started pointing at my crotch! I looked down, and my fly was completely unzipped! Oh my God!

I turned around toward the band and they were falling over laughing.

I pulled up my zipper, shrugged my shoulders and said in the mic, "Well, you all wanted a show you would never forget!" It is one I will never forget.

We used to have a breakfast for my fan club each June at the Opryland Hotel.

Each year, I would raise money for my charities by having an auction. I would bring in personal items and my fans would bid on them. I'd sell my boots, shirts, or a painting.

One year, we were almost out of things to sell and Don Dortch, my manager, stood up and announced, "Folks, now we are going to sell the pants that Ronnie is wearing right now!" I looked at him and thought, "What am I going to wear home?" But the crowd just started going crazy. Then Don said, "And to make it better, Ronnie is going to take them off right here on stage!"

The women started screaming and ran to the stage. But then Don brought out a big blanket, and he and another guy held the blanket up to cover me as I took the pants off. I think the high bid was a few hundred dollars. But I had to walk out of the Opryland Hotel trying to pull my shirt down as low as possible, since I had sold my pants!

Chapter Twenty-One

The Truth

I did some searching in my soul.

When you are writing your life story, you have no trouble sharing all the good times. It is no problem reliving the great times when you were king of the mountain. But when it comes to sharing the bad times… the times that you have wanted to forget… you have a decision to make. My decision was this… Am I going to be completely honest with my fans? Am I going to be completely honest with myself? Am I going to tell the truth?

The next few pages were the hardest to write.

Admitting your biggest mistakes is not easy. Putting them in writing, for all the world to see… is brutal.

So I made my decision. I chose to be honest. To be honest with my fans… with my friends… with my family… and with myself.

Divorce is not pretty.

Especially when you have been together so long.

Divorce is like death.

Karen and I were married more than a quarter of a century.

As soon as Karen and I got married, I started performing at every local club I could book. I would be in Bowling Green, Kentucky, or Lebanon, Tennessee. I was there six nights a week, five shows a night. During those years I started drinking. And I drank too much. I would come home after drinking too much, and Karen would get mad.

I came up with a homemade cure for a hangover. When I needed to get rid of my hangover headache, I would take jello. I would heat it up, and then I'd put ice in it to cool it down, and then I'd drink it. And Karen would make that for me.

We were together more than 26 years. But I wish I would have tried harder and done better. There was too much infidelity on my part. If I could go back and push rewind, and redo all those mistakes that I made...but we can't go back and change things.

The majority of our marriage was tumultuous. There was turmoil. It wasn't pleasant. The real trouble started as soon as the money started pouring in. It happens to a lot of entertainer's spouses. It also happens to doctors' wives, lawyers' wives. You have so much money. But a lot of times, that creates boredom. And that creates depression. And it just escalated every day in our marriage, and it kept getting worse.

I am not perfect. And I know I was a big cause of all that trouble. I know I would have done some things different. We all wish we could go back and change some things.

I wrote a song that goes, "If I could just push rewind, turn back the hands of time. But ya know that's just water under the bridge."

My son Tyler was only seven at the time of our divorce. I got custody of him. Kara, our oldest girl, the divorce was probably the toughest on her. Her and her mama were very close. All our kids were close to their mom.

Our divorce was a long, drawn out process. It actually took four years.

I feel that the best thing a man can do for his children is love their mother. And I wish I had done a better job at that. That would be the biggest thing I would change. I would have tried harder, and done better.

Chapter Twenty-Two

My Kids

The great thing that came out of my marriage to Karen was our kids.

I went to my 10th Class reunion, a short time after I had become a country star. And that night I won the award for having the most kids! I had the most children of anyone in my class.

And I have wonderful kids. I have two daughters. They are both great mamas. They have wonderful families. Kara has two children, Ryan and Sofia. Athena, my youngest daughter, lived with me until she was 30. And she would cry to me at night, "Daddy, no one is going to want me. I'm too old." I said, "Athena, you are 30... and you are beautiful." But she always dated guys who drank beer and hunted deer, and those never worked out. But then she met a banker, and they have three wonderful kids, McCartney, Bellamy and Jovie.

My son Ronnie Dean is a great dad. He has a daughter named Morgan and a son named Garon. All of my grandchildren are little characters.

My youngest son Tyler is waiting until the time is right for him to get married. He's a great guy, and he is so talented. And my son Craig lives in Tulsa. He is a Rap singer. He's got a beautiful daughter, my granddaughter Asia.

I have eight grandkids, and they are all great.

I have always loved being surrounded by my children.

As soon as Ronnie Dean was born, I started taking him on the bus with me. I'd change his diapers on the bus. He was always with me. Tyler was the same way when he came along. The girls were a little bit older when they started coming on the road. But they were still real little. Ronnie Dean could play my song "Love Talks" on the drums when he was seven years old. He started playing for me professionally when he was eighteen. And when he is not playing for me, he is part of Jimmy Buffett's Coral Reefer band.

Tyler got into Al Jolson when he was five years old. I put him on stage with me from that point on. He went from Al Jolson to Michael Jackson to Elvis. In September of 2015, Tyler recorded "The Trump Song", a song I wrote about Donald Trump. He recorded it under the name of TUSK. Tyler can sing anything. He is a great performer.

And now, after raising my sons on stage with me, I am thrilled to be joined on stage by my grandson Garon. Ronnie Dean's son is ten years old. Garon showed an interest in playing the drums when he was eight. He plays a big set of Congas on stage with me. During the summer when he is out of school, he goes out with us. Garon likes to hang out with his Paw Paw. He works out with me. We do P90X workouts, and we go for long walks together.

I always loved my kids, and I always wanted them with me. One time we were at a show and we had thirteen kids on the bus. All of my kids had brought their friends, and my band was so mad! But I loved it! I enjoy having my kids with me.

Chapter Twenty-Three

The Tornado Was Trying To Tell Me Something

My first marriage lasted more than two and a half decades.

My second lasted less than two months. You read it right. Two MONTHS.

I met a girl in Kentucky. We had known each other about two years. Her name was Heather. I met her through a friend of mine.

On a whim, we got married. Our wedding took place on the steps of the Stockyards Restaurant in Nashville. Why we got married there, I have no idea. During the ceremony, it was storming so bad, we thought a tornado was coming through. That should have told me something. It was a crazy day, and it kind of summed up our marriage.

The final straw came the day I got home to find her waiting for me at the door.

She had her cell phone in her hand and yelled at me, "Did you give a gift to a girl from Lexington?" I said, "What are you talking about?"

I came to find out that the gift I gave happened in the late 70s.

I told her, "If you are going to live in my past, you cannot live in my present." She took off walking, and I have not seen her since!

Chapter Twenty-Four

Jamie

After my two month marriage, I decided that it would be a long time before I looked to get into another relationship. I really had no desire to get involved with anyone.

Then I met Jamie.

I met Jamie on a cruise. She was there with her mom. Her mama was doing a pre-cruise party, and I was performing. Jamie and her mom were standing there, and I walked up and talked to her mom for a minute and I asked to borrow a pen. When I left, her mom asked her if she knew who I was. She didn't. After my show, Jamie was walking by, and I grabbed her arm and said, "Hey, you're coming with me." And we've been together ever since. At the time, she lived in West Monroe, Louisiana. For a year, every weekend she would make that nine hour trip to Nashville. She made that drive on Friday night, and then made the nine hour trip back home on Sunday. She finally got tired of that and she moved up here.

Of course Jamie is much younger than me. But that was not the thing that attracted me to her. It was her smile. She smiled all the time. I have never seen her not smiling. I love people who are happy, and I love someone who cuts up and laughs. And Jamie and I laugh all the time. We are friends. She puts my vitamins out every day. She runs my bath water for me each night. She is a needle in the haystack. I am so thankful I found her.

We have been together for three years. We don't know what the future holds. But we do know that we love each other.

Chapter Twenty-Five

"Yes, He Is Your Kid"

Remember a few chapters back and my decision to be honest?

The honesty continues...

In 1980, I was playing at a club called Ziegfeld's. I was separated at the time. And I had a one night stand. A short time after that, I started to hear whispers about how she may have gotten pregnant. But I never really heard anything about it.

Then about eight years ago, a woman contacted a friend of mine and said she was going to put a story about me in a newspaper. My friend gave me the woman's phone number and I called her. She said, "My husband is your son, and he cries all the time because you won't have anything to do with him." I said, "How can I have anything to do with him if I didn't know he exists?" I said, "Put him on the phone. I want to talk to him." When he picked up the phone, I said, "Craig, why do you think I'm your dad?" He said, "Because I am a dead ringer for you." We spoke quite a while, and I said, "I need to talk to your mother." So he gave me her number and I called her. Jennifer was a captain in the Army. She had just gotten back from Iraq. And we talked and she said, "Yes, he is your kid."

I agreed to take a blood test. When we got the results, I went straight to all my kids and told them. And to be honest, they were kind of excited about meeting him. So we set up a meeting in St Louis. I took my son Tyler along. And when Craig walked in, he spread his arms and said, "Hey, my brother from another mother!" They looked like twins! It was absolutely amazing how much they looked alike. Craig has a little daughter, Asia, who is my granddaughter. She is smart as a tack.

Chapter Twenty-Six

My Musical Family

I have had the honor of working with so many talented people over the years. Not only have I been able to make a good living while doing what I love to do, but I have also had the chance to become friends with many of my musical heroes.

Here are some of my thoughts, and a few "behind the scenes" stories about some of those friends:

Carl Perkins - I did a show in Portland, Tennessee on the football field. Carl Perkins came to that show, and I couldn't believe he was there.

I got to be with him over the years after that. He always told me great Elvis stories. He told me the first time he and Elvis met, he asked Elvis "Hey, are you wearing eye makeup?" This was 1955, and men did not wear eye makeup unless you were Liberace. And Elvis answered him, "Yeah man, it brings out my eyes."

Carl and his brothers were old farm boys, and after Elvis left, Carl's brother said, "He ain't as pretty as he thinks he is." And Carl said, "I don't know. He's pretty damn pretty!"

Tammy Wynette – Tammy Wynette had the most unique voice. Her voice would break at certain little places. It was so special. I was just crazy about all her songs.

Tammy was one of the sweetest people I have ever met. Just humble and down to earth. One of the things I have discovered is the bigger the star, the more humble and nicer they are.

Loretta Lynn - I met Loretta Lynn for the first time at an awards show. Then I got to know her as we did shows with Conway.

Now when I look back at those years, I think... I got to be on stage with Conway and Loretta. It don't get no better than that. Loretta Lynn is one of the kindest, sweetest people in the world.

John Conlee - The first time I met John Conlee was when I took "The King is Gone" to the big rock station in Nashville. The DJ said, "You have got a smash." That DJ was John Conlee.

Of course, he stopped playing records on the radio when he started recording big hit records of his own. John has one of the most unique voices in music.

We have worked many shows together. He did a show for my Children's Cancer Foundation.

Mickey Gilley - I was a big Mickey Gilley fan before I ever met him. I played his theater in Branson quite a bit.

I taped the "Country Family Reunion" TV show, and Mickey was on the show. During a break, Mickey pulled me aside and said, "Ronnie, you are a true entertainer." And coming from him, that is a huge compliment.

Jerry Lee Lewis - Jerry Lee Lewis is one of the wildest, craziest humans on the planet.

I got to know Jerry Lee very well. I did two songs with him. We did the classic "Heartaches By The Number", and another song that I wrote called "A Little Past 40."

Of course, Jerry Lee started out at Sun Records, just after Elvis. Many people think that Jerry Lee didn't like Elvis' success overshadowing his. But Elvis overshadowed everyone!

Less than a year before Elvis died, Jerry Lee was arrested at the gates of Graceland. He was drunk and he had a gun. People have always wondered exactly what was going on.

After I got to know him, I asked him, "Jerry Lee, that night you went up and busted through the gates of Graceland with that gun... what the hell were you thinking?" He said, "Well, you see killer... I was tired of being number two... and I was gonna shoot him." Jerry Lee smiled real big after he said that, so I still do not know if he was serious or not.

But I will say this about Jerry Lee Lewis... as wild and crazy as he is... he's got a good heart. A lot of people don't think that. But Jerry Lee has a good heart. He really does.

Dolly Parton - The first time I met Dolly, her manager called me and told me Dolly had written a song called "Last Night I Dreamed About Elvis." And she wanted me to sing a line from her song "I Will Always Love You" in that new song with her.

When we went to record it in the studio, we were talking about how large our families were. She said, "My mother had a dozen kids to take care of. We ended up putting her on a pedestal." I said "What do you mean?" She said, "We put mama up on a pedestal to keep daddy off of her!"

I did a painting of Dolly and Elvis. I gave it to her and she screamed with joy. She is the sweetest woman. I asked her if I could get her permission to sell prints of the painting. And she said, "Ronnie, you make all the money you want." As I said earlier: the bigger the star, the nicer they are.

Jimmy Fortune - In my opinion, Jimmy Fortune is the BEST singer out there. He is the very best. His writing and his singing... his voice cuts like a knife.

Jimmy is the most humble person. He reminds me of Keith Whitley. He was the most gentle, sweetest spirited man I have ever known.

George Jones - I was on a show with Tammy Wynette, George Jones, and Larry Gatlin and the Gatlin Brothers. I was so thrilled to be on a show with George Jones. He was one of my all-time heroes. But after I did my part of the show, Tammy came out on stage, took the mic, and said, "I hate to tell you all this, but George is not here tonight. He is at a little bar... performing for the folks there." I thought, "you have got to be kidding me."

But I got to meet him the next day on a plane. And I ended up getting to know him very well over the years. I will never forget when I picked up the phone and the voice at the other end said, "Yeah Ronnie, this is George Jones. And I want you to do a painting of me getting a DUI on my lawn mower."

That is one of the most famous incidents George's life during his drinking years. Tammy had taken all his car keys away, and he took off on a riding mower to go to the liquor store.

So I did the painting and I had just finished it. On Christmas Day, the phone rang. It was George, and he asked me to bring it over to their house. I told him, "But George, it is Christmas day." He said, "What better day?" So I was wearing a Santa hat when I walked in his front door. When I took the cover off of the painting, he stood and looked at it for 30 minutes. I will never forget that huge smile that I gave George Jones on that Christmas day.

A couple months later, he called and asked me to re-do the painting. He said he looked too old in the first one. I had already sold the original for $25,000. I had already sold five hundred prints. So I got to thinking, "if I re-do it, I will have a new original and new prints to sell". So I did a new version, this one with an older police car and older John Deere mower, and I made George younger, with that classic flat top haircut.

George asked me to come to his 80th birthday party. I took the new painting and he said, "Son, you got it right this time." Now that painting is in the George Jones Museum in Nashville.

Billy Joe Royal - Billy Joe Royal was a piece of work. Billy was one of my best friends. He was one of the sweetest, kindest and most laidback people I have ever known.

On the song "Down in the Boondocks", he sang higher than a girl. A lot of people thought it was a girl. He still sang just like that, right up until the day he died.

When I met Billy, I found that he was so humble. He was a guy you would pick to be your friend. I never heard him raise his voice.

We had a show in Seattle, and Billy hated flying. When we were getting on the plane he said, "I took four Xanax and still couldn't sleep last night." He was so nervous. He never calmed down the entire flight. We got to Seattle with no problem. We did our show and I jokingly said, "So, are you ready to get back on the Buddy Holly Express?" He said, "Why did you say that?" I said, "I'm just joking." But it didn't matter. He wouldn't get on the plane. The next day, he rented a car and drove all the way back to Nashville!

Billy always did his hair like Donald Trump. I told him, "You need a different hairstyle." My daughter-in-law is a hairstylist, and I told him to go to her. And it looked unbelievable. I told him, "Don't ever let anybody but my daughter-in-law do your hair!"

Billy was one of my heroes. I spoke to him just a few days before he died. I would call him to check on him, and to tell him I loved him. I miss him dearly. He died way too soon. He really did burn like a rocket!

Roy Acuff - I still have the knife Roy Acuff gave me. He had a house at Opryland, inside the theme park. It was just a short walk from the TNN

TV studios. Roy was watching me one night on "Nashville Now" with Ralph Emery. I was talking about how much I loved him, and he just walked over and gave me a knife.

Bill Medley - I watched Bill on the old TV show "Shindig". I never dreamed I would get to meet or work with Bill Medley. But we struck up a friendship from the moment we met.

When the Righteous Brothers were playing Las Vegas, Elvis would surprise them by walking out on stage in the middle of their show. And not only did that surprise the Righteous Brothers, but it blew away the audience! They just went crazy. There is no gentler, nicer person than Bill Medley. He is the most humble guy.

T Graham Brown - T Graham is one of the funniest guys you will ever meet. He is also one of the greatest singers on the planet.

We did shows when he first started. And today we still do many shows together. I hire him myself to be on the bill with me.

He is nice, but his wife is actually nicer than him. I'm just kiddin', T! They are both wonderful, kind, loving people.

I did an album, and I asked him to do a duet with me. He came in wearing house slippers, and it looked like he had pajamas on. I said "Thanks for dressing up!" But he did such an amazing job on the song. He walked out of the studio and said, "Now, let's see you top that."

He is one of the best people in the world.

T.G. Sheppard - Buddy Killen was producing T.G. Sheppard at the same time he was producing me.

T.G. has told me so many Elvis stories. Of course Elvis helped him get his first bus. T.G. has invited me his Christmas parties. If you go to one of those, it is like a who's who. There is everyone from Dave Ramsey to Ralph Emery to Barry Gibb.

T.G. is married to Kelly Lang, and I have known Kelly for years. Kelly's dad worked for Conway Twitty, and her dad and I were buddies when I was touring with Conway. We have all been friends for 40 years.

Eddy Raven - Eddy Raven is one of the best singers around, still to this day. A great singer, great entertainer. I have booked Eddy to be on a lot of my shows, because I love him so much.

Little Richard - I met Little Richard in Woodland Studios. That's where I recorded all my very early stuff. The first thing Little Richard said to me was, "I can tell you're one of God's children." And he preached to me the whole time.

Later, I was working at the Horseshoe Casino in Tunica, Mississippi. And Little Richard was going to be there the night before me, in the same show room. And I was able to take my sister Tutti to meet him. We were going to meet him after the show. But during the show, Tutti actually got up on stage and was going toward him when his bodyguards took her off stage. Afterward, I said, "What were you doing?" She said, "I just had to touch him!"

But I was able to take her backstage, and I told him that my sister used to buy all his records at Randy's Record Shop in Gallatin, Tennessee and she loved him so much. So much that her nickname was Tutti, after his big song Tutti Frutti. And when they met, she ran over and hugged him, and she whispered something in his ear. To this day, she will not tell me what she whispered to Little Richard.

George Strait - I worked with George Strait a lot. George hadn't really hit that big yet, and he was on the bill with me and Conway.

I co-wrote a song called "Under These Conditions". Me, Joe Meador and Troy Seals wrote that. Conway had told me that if I ever wanted to write a great song, that I needed to write with Troy Seals. Troy wrote "Don't Take It Away" for Conway. He also wrote a song called "Rock N' Roll Heart" that was a hit for Eric Clapton. I did a remake of that and turned it into "Country Boy's Heart". Troy Seals is one of the greatest guys on the planet, and he's one of the greatest songwriters.

All the songs I wrote, I wrote for Tree Publishing. And George Strait would go to Tree himself, and listen to songs himself. He didn't send someone to do it for him. That's why I love George. He would go listen to the songs himself.

And he liked our song "Under These Conditions", and he put it on his "If You Ain't Lovin', You Ain't Livin'" album in 1988. That was right when George was becoming a superstar. That album had three number ones, the title track, "Baby Blue", and "Famous Last Words Of A Fool."

The album went platinum almost instantly, and just kept selling.

Even though our song was not released as a single, anytime you write a song that's on an album that goes double or triple quadruple platinum, the residuals will go to your grandkids and great grandkids... they just keep coming.

Faron Young - Faron Young was one of the kindest people I have ever met. But he was one of the craziest.

I was having lunch with him one day. And a woman came over to the table and said, "Mr. Young, can I have your autograph?" Faron yelled at her, "Can't you see that I'm eating?! If you will go over there and set your ass down, when I get done I will sign your autograph!" I sat there thinking, "Oh my Lord." But she went over, sat down and waited. And as soon as Faron finished eating, he went over and signed her autograph!

Tom Jones - I met Tom Jones at a club named "Barbara's" in Printer's Alley in Nashville. We got to visit for two hours. My first words to Tom Jones were "Tom, you are my second favorite singer!" And in his Welch brogue, he said, "Who the hell is your first favorite?"

Tom told me a great Elvis story. Elvis was visiting Tom in his dressing room. And Tom was taking a shower. And Elvis kept looking into the shower at Tom. And Tom finally said, "Let's talk after I get out of the shower."

The Drifters - I love The Drifters. We all grew up with their songs like "Under The Boardwork", "On Broadway", "Save The Last Dance For Me" and "This Magic Moment".

A lot of those songs were written by Doc Pomas and Mort Shuman.

In my early days, I played in New York at the Lone Star café, and Doc Pomas used to come see me. I was a huge Doc Pomas fan. He wrote "Suspicion", which was one of my favorite Elvis songs. And I couldn't believe Doc would come see me. He was in a wheelchair at the time. But I was honored to sing "Suspicion" for him.

Bill Pinkney, who was one of the original Drifters, died on the 4th of July, 2007. But one time, we were traveling together. We were driving down the road and, as he drove, he pulled out a big, long hunter's knife and he dry-shaved his face with that knife as he drove!

I ended up doing an album with The Drifters. It is one my favorite things I've done.

Wayne Newton - I did a song with Wayne Newton. In 1977, I went to see one of Wayne's concerts, and he blew me away. Years later, I was honored to do a duet with Wayne. Mike Curb wrote the song "Saturday Night Special" for me and Wayne. It was not a huge hit, but I was still thrilled to sing with "Mr. Las Vegas."

Jerry Reed - I was in a limousine with Jerry Reed, and he told me about his first meeting with Elvis.

Jerry wrote "U.S. Male" and "Guitar Man", which were two really great songs. Elvis used them both in his Comeback Special.

But Elvis also loved Jerry's guitar playing, and he wanted him on his session. When Jerry got there, he couldn't take his eyes off Elvis. He just stared at him. And Elvis told him, "Hey man, you are making me uncomfortable. You got to quit staring at me." And Jerry said, "I can't help it. You are the prettiest sumbitch I have ever seen!"

Exile - Exile should have been the biggest thing in country music! They should have been bigger than the group Alabama. I love Alabama. All of Alabama are my friends, but Exile should have been bigger. Les, Sonny, Marlon, J.P. and Steve are the most talented people I have ever known.

Buddy Killen produced Exile when he was producing me. And as we all worked together, I found that not only were they talented, but they were just unbelievable human beings.

J.P. Pennington is one of the greatest songwriters there has ever been. And he's one of the greatest singers and pickers. J.P. helped me write the song "A Little Past 40". J.P., me and Buddy Killen wrote that song. It didn't do a lot here in the U.S., but it was the number one song of the year in Denmark. I tried to copy some of J.P.'s attitude and style in that song.

You will never meet a nicer group of guys than Exile.

Ray Price - I was doing a show with Ray Price in Silver Springs, Florida. I walked onto his bus and the smoke was so thick. He was smoking a joint. I said, "Mr. Price, that doesn't bother your throat?" He said, "No Ronnie, this is what helps me sing!"

He had the most incredible, beautiful voice. At the end of his life, he sounded as good or better than he did 50 years ago.

Charlie Chase/Lorianne Crook - I got to know Charlie Chase when he was doing the news on the local Nashville TV station.

I met Jim Owens, Lorianne's husband, shortly after "The King is Gone" hit. Jim always believed in me, and always tried to help me. He was the producer of so many TV shows. Just about any TV show that was on at the time, Jim either was the producer of it, or he played a big role of some kind. And he would always have me on his shows.

When Charlie and Lorriane did the "Music City Tonight" nightly show on The Nashville Network, they called and asked me to be a regular on their show, and I did that for two years. That helped draw huge crowds to my concerts, because they saw me on TV each night.

I also learned how to play to the TV camera on those shows. I learned where and when to look at the camera, so I could connect to the folks who were watching at home.

The Oak Ridge Boys - I was in Portland, Oregon with The Oak Ridge Boys.

Joe Bonsall walked up to me and said, "Ronnie, you need to come out and watch us do this new song. It's a Dallas Frazier song, and the roof is just coming off of everyplace as soon as we sing it." I said, "What is the name of it?" Joe said, "Elvira!"

That night, I was standing just off stage when they started singing "Elvira", and when Richard Sterban hit those low notes, "Giddy up a oom papa mow mow", the crowd went nuts!

The Oaks also sang on a song I recorded called "Oh How Happy." They are as humble as anyone you will ever meet.

Ferlin Husky - Ferlin Husky loved my version of "Gone", which was a huge hit for him.

Ferlin called me and told me they were inducting him into the Country Music Hall of Fame. And he said he wanted me to sing "Gone" at that ceremony. I was flabbergasted. I said, "Are you sure you want me to sing your song?" He said, "Son, you are the only one I want doing it."

At the induction ceremony, The Jordanaires joined me on stage. Gordon Stoker was still alive. Millie Kirkham was there. Millie and Gordon sang on Ferlin's original record in 1957.

I went to Gordon and said, "Gordon, I can't believe I am getting to sing this song with you and Millie." He said, "Yeah, all the rest who were on that record are dead… and I'm not feeling too damn hot myself!"

Ferlin was sitting in the front row. He had oxygen tubes in his nose, IVs in his arms. He was in a wheelchair. As soon as I started the song, I leaped off the stage and went down to Ferlin, and we sang that song together. Until the day I die, that will be one of the biggest thrills of my life.

  Jeff Bates - Jeff Bates sounds so much like Conway Twitty. He does Conway Twitty better than Conway did it! Jeff had a tough time over the years, but has really turned his life completely around and is just a wonderful person. We did a fundraiser together in October of 2015, and I asked him to do Elvis' "Suspicious Minds" with me. He asked what key we would do it in. I told him, "Elvis' key." He said, "That is high for me." But he did great. He also did "American Trilogy" with me. Jeff is a great guy.

The fans went wild and I loved it.

My early band. Ricky, Tommy, Ronnie, Doug, Ernie

SCORPION
RECORDS

RONNIE McDOWELL
& THE NASHVILLE ROAD

Road Mgr.
MIKE ROWLAND
502-586-6179

SCORPION RECORDS

RONNIE McDOWELL

RONNIE McDOWELL FAN CLUB
P.O. BOX 711
MADISON, TENN. 37115

 Ronnie McDowell

MANAGEMENT:
BETTER TALENT, INC.
38 MUSIC SQUARE E.
NASHVILLE, TENN. 37203
(615) 256-3373

Little Nashville Indiana Nov. 1979

Just a little of the Elvis sideburn

"Please no pictures"…words I never said.

Having fun with my fans

With a beard in Hagerstown MD, 1980. Courtesy Betty Moody

The things publicity people make you do!

With my daughter Kara

My family: Ronnie Dean, Karne, Tyler, Ronnie, Athena, Kara

Courtesy Joe Meador collection

With Ralph Emery on Nashville

Filming the music video "I Don't Want To Set The World On Fire"

Always wondering what Jerry Lee Lewis would do next!

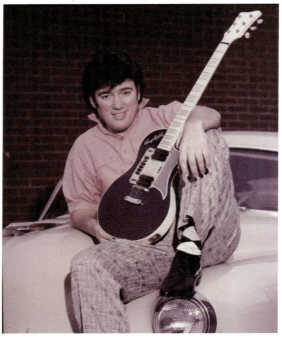

Courtesy Joe Meador

With my friend Pat Boone

With D.J. Fontana in Elvis' Audubon Dr. home.   Courtesy Mike Payne

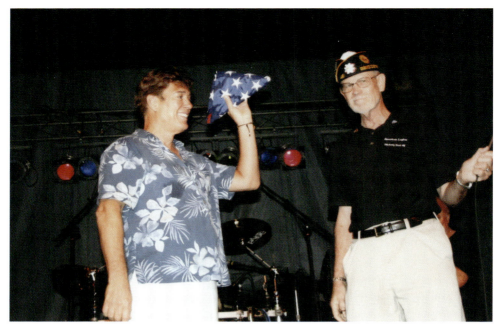
The American Legion presenting me with a flag for my service.
Courtesy Allen Coker

Singing for just a few of my closest friends.   *Courtesy Alan Mayor*

Chapter Twenty-Seven

My Fans... My Friends

I am so thankful for my fans.

Many of them have been supporting me for almost 40 years!

They come from all over the country to see my shows. They'll drive for 500, 600, 700 miles. They will sit in the rain. It amazes me.

In return, I have spent many a night or early morning visiting with my fans at the local Waffle House after a concert. I don't know how many other artists do that. But I would suggest it to any of them, as I always get as much or more out of it as my fans do.

I had an International Fan Club. It was headquartered in Richland Station in downtown Portland, Tennessee. We had a restaurant and our offices there.

We also had so many people who wanted to have their own fan club for their own state. At one time, I had more than thirty fan clubs. Each state had its own Ronnie McDowell fan club chapter.

And when you combine all those, at one time, I had the third-biggest fan club in the world. It was bigger than Loretta Lynn's, which was really the one that started all of the fan clubs.

Wanda Myrick has been running my fan club for 30 years. She has done it without any compensation. Wanda is from Russellville, Alabama, and she is the biggest Elvis fan on the planet. You had better not say anything negative about Elvis around Wanda. She saw Elvis in person six times.

I met Wanda in 1977. A friend asked her to go with them to one of my concerts, and Wanda told them, "No, I do not want to see an Elvis impersonator." But they talked her into going, and it didn't take her long to find out I was not an impersonator.

Soon after that, Wanda started a Ronnie McDowell Fan Club chapter in Alabama, and she later became my National Fan Club Coordinator. She is probably the single most, hardest working person that I have had in my career. Wanda has done everything she could for me. She has done everything from babysit my children on the bus to iron my clothes before a show.

I know that Wanda loves me. She is not "in love" with me, but she loves me. And I love her. I will always be thankful for her.

I have gotten to know many of my fans over the years. I have gotten close to them over the last four decades. They were there when I started, and they have stuck with me all those years. I have a few fans who have been with me so long that they have become like family to me. They are like my sisters. They have been so supportive. A few that come to mind… Linda and Connie in North Carolina. Melissa in North Carolina, as well. I have a Cheri and a Sherry in Illinois. They have been with me since day one. Nancy and Darlene have been coming to my shows and supporting me since 1977. Cindy ran my Illinois Fan Club for 20 years. I thank her and all the fans who ran my fan clubs in all the different states. And I thank the fans who now run my internet fan clubs and fan websites. Those folks do all that work for one reason…they care about me. And I love them .

I've watched my fans go from young, unmarried people, to being married, to being mothers, to being grandparents. They bring their kids to the shows, and now their kids are bringing their kids. I think that's wonderful. It's great.

There is one very special gal, Barbara Rippy. When I met her in Las Vegas, she was 43 years old. Now she's in her 80s. And she might be the all-time biggest Ronnie McDowell fan.

I met Barbara Rippy in 1977 in Greenville, South Carolina. We met again the next year, when Barbara and Connie Lockabee came to a huge Elvis convention in Las Vegas.

Barbara and her husband Bobby operated a drug store in Union, South Carolina.

Bobby was such a good man. He let Barbara travel all over the world to see me. She has been to hundreds of my concerts. It's possible that she has seen more than 1,000 of my shows. She followed me from town to town. She paid to bring me to her hometown of Union, South Carolina for concerts there more than a half dozen times.

And when I say she followed us, I mean it. She would drive right behind our bus. We joked that she had gotten hooked on diesel fumes. She smelled a lot of the diesel fumes from our tour bus!

In 1978, Barbara was planning to go to Las Vegas. Before she left home, her husband told her, "Don't you get hooked on those slot machines." She said, "We are going to shows every night. I won't have time for any gambling."

Well, halfway through her stay in Vegas, Barbara was completely broke! She had started playing those slot machines and couldn't stop. She had to call her husband and ask him to wire money for her to get home! She never went back to Vegas.

Every time we had a charity auction, Barbara bought everything. She has a huge Ronnie McDowell collection, everything from my guitars to my stage outfits. She has spent thousands of dollars at my auctions, with the money going to my charities.

One time Barbara drove a long, long way to come to one of my shows. It was far. I had Tyler Dean with me, and he was real little at the time. When we got to the venue, I saw that it was a smoky nightclub. I didn't want to take Tyler in, but I didn't have anyone to stay with him.

So when Barbara got there to pick up her tickets, I asked her if she would mind staying on the bus to take care of Tyler. And she did that. She had just driven hundreds of miles and she didn't even get to see my show!

But she did it with a smile. Now that is not just a fan. That is a friend... a dear friend.

As a thank you for all the years of her supporting me, I did a painting as a surprise for Barbara. I redid the famous Norman Rockwell Pharmacy picture. And since Barbara and her husband operated a drug store, I painted her husband as the pharmacist, and I also put Barbara in the painting When I gave it to her, she cried and cried and cried.

A funny thing happened with Barbara. She always had a saying when she saw me. She would say, "Who is my #1?" And I'd say "Ronnie McDowell."

One year at Fan Fair, a CNN reporter came up to Barbara and asked, "Who are you listening to these days?" And Barbara completely froze up! She stood there looking at the TV camera and finally said, "Wade Hayes"!

I called her and said, "Barbara, the only time you could have given me worldwide attention... on CNN... and you said Wade Hayes?!"

After that, when she would come to my shows, she would ask, "Who is my #1?" and I would say, "Well, I guess it is Wade Hayes!"

Quite a while after that, Barbara had a brain aneurysm. She was not expected to live. No one lives through what she had. I took my bus and went to the hospital in South Carolina. I leaned down and kissed her, and she ended up coming out of that brain aneurysm, and she lives today. And she's probably listening to Wade Hayes right now!

Chapter Twenty-Eight

Truth Is Stranger Than Fiction

I was doing a show in Tunica, Mississippi, about an hour south of Memphis.

I had a new car, and I had never operated the GPS system in the car. But I punched in "Nashville" in the GPS, and took off toward home.

As I drove into Memphis, I knew I was headed in the wrong direction, but I didn't know how to change the GPS. So I thought I would just follow the instructions and see what happened. I drove a little further, and then the GPS voice said, "You have reached your destination." I stopped the car and looked out the window, and I was parked at 1034 Audubon Drive... the exact house Elvis bought in 1956! This was the home he lived in before he bought Graceland.

That is the strangest thing that has ever happened to me. I know that Elvis was trying to tell me something. But I still haven't figured out what it is.

As I looked at Elvis' former home, I kept hearing that GPS saying, "You have reached your destination..."

Chapter Twenty-Nine

My Elvis Family

One of the most amazing things about my career and my life... is the fact that I have been able to work with, and become friends with, almost every person who was ever connected with Elvis. I treasure the true and lasting friendships I have made with every one of those people.

I have worked with some of those folks almost as long as Elvis was alive. I have been working with The Jordanaires for almost 40 years, and Elvis only lived 42 years. I've known George Klein and Red West almost the same amount of time.

I never got to meet Elvis, so I am very humbled that those who knew him the very best have allowed me to be a part of their family.

Here are some memories about a few of my Elvis friends:

Sam Phillips - Of course, Sam Phillips was the founder of Sun Records. If it weren't for him, the world may have never heard of Elvis Presley.

I was doing a show in Memphis, and Sam came to see me. He got there real early in the afternoon so he could visit with Scotty Moore and the other guys.

Sam got there about 2:00, and by the time the show started, he had already killed two bottles of wine.

Halfway through the show, I went down in the audience and gave Sam this huge introduction, and then I said, "Mr. Phillips, would you like to say a few words?"

He grabbed that microphone out of my hand and took it in both of his hands and started talking. And (with help from those two bottles of wine) he went on a tirade that I could not stop! He talked for almost 20 minutes, and he didn't really say anything!

I kept waiting for a place where I could jump in. And finally, Sam paused to cough. Man, I grabbed that mic and took off... much to the relief of the audience!

Sam and I became real close over the years. He was just one of my best friends ever. He did things for me that he wouldn't do for anyone else. I did a video at Tootsie's on Broadway in Nashville, and he came and sat on a stool for three hours while we filmed. Later, his son told me, "Ronnie, he wouldn't do that for nobody but you. That shows you how much he loves you."

Priscilla Presley - Priscilla is just a lovely person. I can see why Elvis fell for her. She has done so much for me and my career over the years. She has been such a supporter of mine. The first time I met Priscilla, the first words she said were, "Do you have any idea what you have done for Elvis?" She was always very sweet and kind to me.

That same day, I was visiting with Kris Kristofferson. Kris was also at Graceland, and he came over to me and said, "Ronnie, I feel like we are standing on hallowed ground." I thought, "Kris Kristofferson is one of the greatest songwriters of our time. He is a music legend and he's a movie star. When someone like that says the property around your house is hallowed ground... wow... Elvis was HUGE."

Scotty Moore - Scotty Moore was there at the beginning with Elvis. It was Elvis, Scotty, and Bill Black. They were the ones who started it all.

But I ended up working much longer with Scotty than Elvis did. We have done thousands of shows together. I am thankful for our friendship. He is one of my very closest and dearest friends.

One time when we were on tour, Scotty had passed out after drinking Johnnie Walker Red. It was dark on the bus, and my daughter didn't see him laying on the couch, and she sat on his head!

I love Scotty. And I know he loves me. He showed that love when he gave me a priceless gift.

The first time Elvis was on TV, he was on the Dorsey show. And he had a great watch that he wore during his first television appearance. It was a 1956 Elgin watch. And he ended up giving it to Scotty Moore.

Scotty kept that watch for decades, and for Christmas in 1994, he gave that watch to me. I stood there and cried.

But ten years later, I gave Scotty a gift he would never forget. Elvis gave away close to 200 cars. But it always bothered me that he never gave one to Scotty Moore or D.J. Fontana. Heck, Scotty's wife's car was the original car they used when they toured for the first time. They wore that car out, and Bobbie never got her car back!

So I found a 1953 Chevy Bel Air. I had it painted the same color as the one Scotty and D.J. drove when they were with Elvis. And I gave Scotty and D.J. that car on the 50th Anniversary of the recording of "That's Alright Mama."

D.J. said, "I am gonna have a heart attack. Nobody has ever gave me a car."

George Klein - Of all of the Elvis folks I have worked with, one of my closest friends is George Klein.

George was the M.C. of a show I did when I was opening for Jerry Lee Lewis and Hank Williams, Jr. After that, George always told the folks at Graceland that they should get me for any big events they were doing.

During many of my concerts, I like to pick someone from the audience to help me sing a song. One night George was in the audience, so I went out to him. I quickly found out he couldn't sing a lick! And that made me want to always try to put him on the spot, when he came to any of my shows!

I have an inside joke with George. When he gets up on stage, I tell everyone he is a tenor. Here's the story behind that…

George would be with Elvis at Graceland. Elvis loved to gather his friends around the piano and sing gospel songs.

George would be there with The Stamps Quartet and J.D. Sumner, and they'd all be singing. About halfway through a song, Elvis held up his hand and said, "Whoa, whoa… G.K. (Elvis always called him G.K.), you need to lay out and not sing."

George said, "E, you don't like my singing?"

Elvis said "You can sing Tenor."

George asked, "Tenor what?"

Elvis laughed, "Ten or fifteen miles down the road!"

The reason Elvis Presley loved George Klein is because George never took one thing from Elvis. George told him, "Elvis, I don't want your things. I just want your friendship." I treasure my friendship with George.

D.J. Fontana - D.J. Fontana was Elvis' original drummer. He was there to help the rocketship blast off.

D.J. played on a lot of my recording sessions. We always had a great time. I was honored to be in the studio with him and Scotty Moore, and all those legends. And to get to know them all and become friends with them, that was just a dream come true.

I have been able to become very best friends with D.J. over the years. We have done hundreds of concerts together. I would always say, "D.J., I love you." And he'd just grunt or wouldn't say anything. And one day I finally said, "D.J., I'm not leaving here until you tell me you love me." His wife Karen said, "If you can get him to say that to you, you are really doing something. He doesn't ever tell me that." But he finally said to me, "I love ya." And now, after all of our shows, he tells me he loves me.

In 2004, D.J. and Scotty Moore were doing a show with me in Tunica, Mississippi. I asked them both to go outside with me. As we stepped out, there were two cars parked there. I handed D.J. a key, and then I handed a key to Scotty. I gave them each a new car.

I had actually asked all of my friends in the music business to contribute to the cars. Ray Stevens gave me six hundred dollars and The Rolling Stones donated $3,500!

I gave Scotty a new Ford Explorer. I was going to give him a Cadillac, but I knew he would like the Explorer better. And I gave D.J. a new Cadillac.

June Juanico - In the 1950s, I saw photos of Elvis in the movie magazines. And he was always with this beautiful girl. She was his first girlfriend. Her name was June Juanico. I was just a little boy, but I looked at their pictures and thought, "What a pretty girl."

As I grew up, I often wondered what happened to that beautiful girl.

After I had hit it big, I was playing at the Imperial Palace in Biloxi, Mississippi. And I was going to a party at the steakhouse there. As I was walking in, I saw this pretty woman greeting people. She had gray hair.

I told her, "I know you. But I don't know where we have met." Then I looked at her name tag and it said "June". And right at that moment, I knew... this was June Juanico, Elvis' first girlfriend! I gave her a big hug and we have been close friends ever since.

June had actually come to see one of my shows a year before I met her.

After we became friends, I gave June a painting I did. It was of her and Elvis when they were teenagers. As she looked at it, she just started crying. She said it brought back so many memories.

She has been asked about Elvis and her relationship with him all of her life, but she doesn't mind. June loves Elvis' fans.

June and I spent an entire Easter Sunday together one year. We had a catfish dinner on Easter. Even today, June still has a lot of fire in her furnace.

And all these years later, I can honestly say that I can see why Elvis fell for June.

I love her dearly.

Gene/Louise Smith - I was doing a show with Carl Perkins at Mud Island. Ray Walker of the Jordanaires introduced me to Gene and Louise Smith. Gene was Elvis' first cousin, but they were really as close as brothers.

Gene went on the road with Elvis during his very early years. Elvis' mother Gladys told Gene to always make Elvis Light Bread. That was two pieces of bread with fried potatoes and mustard. My family also ate Light Bread. It was really good. Of course, we fried the potatoes in lard! That's what made it good. When they were teenagers, Elvis wanted to date Louise, but she liked Gene better. She said Elvis was too cocky and was always combing his hair. Gene asked her out, and on their very first date, when she went to get in the car, Elvis was sitting in the back seat with his guitar! Gene told her, "I don't go anywhere without 'cuz."

From the moment we met, Gene, Louise and I became the best of friends. They would stay at my house when they came to Nashville.

Gene died in 1999, but Louise and I have stayed very close. Any time I play in Tunica, I always stop to visit her in Memphis. If she ever needs anything, she knows all she has to do is call me.

Louise has told me that after her two sons, I am the next most important man in her life. Today, Louise Smith is like my mama. She is like my second mother. I just love her to death. She is one great, true friend. There is no better person in the world.

The Jordanaires - One of the most important groups in musical history. They sang background on all of Elvis' records for fifteen years. On everything from "Heartbreak Hotel" to "Hound Dog", the group that was singing all of those "Bop, bop, bop, bops" behind Elvis was The Jordanaires.

In 1978, I did a tour with all of the original members of The Jordanaires. The first thing I wanted to do when I started recording was to have the Jordanaires back me up on my records. On my second record, The Jordanaires name was on the record. It was billed as "Ronnie McDowell with The Jordanaires". What a thrill to have them want to work with me. They sang on "Wandering Eyes", "Watching Girls Go By", "Older Women".

I have had the great honor of working with The Jordanaires many more years than Elvis did. We have done hundreds of concerts together.

Later, Gordon Stoker's sons both came to me and said, "You'll never know what you have done for our dad. Getting him back on stage really gave him a new sense of purpose." I am honored and humbled to say that The Jordanaires loved me... not as a singer, but as a person.

J.D. Sumner - The first time I met J.D. Sumner was in Peoria, Illinois. Elvis had just died. "The King is Gone" was huge, so they put me on the show with J.D. Sumner and the Stamps.

Before the show, Ed Enoch of the Stamps came to me and told me J.D. wanted to see me. Me being the big Elvis fan I was, I was excited to meet J.D. He was one of my heroes. I had loved him forever. But the moment I walked on the bus, J.D.'s first words to me... in the very deep, slow voice... were, "Son, I'm gonna kick your ass."

I said, "What did I do?"

J.D. said, "Son, I don't think I should be opening for you. How do I go from singing with the biggest star of all time to opening a show for you. You only have one song."

By then, I realized J.D. was a little inebriated. I told him, "I would rather go on first anyway. It would be an honor for me to open for you and the Stamps."

He sat there a minute and said, "I'm sorry I talked to you that way. I apologize to you, Ronnie. Forgive me. I've been having a little drink here."

I said, "You don't have to apologize." And from that moment on, J.D. was the nicest, kindest person you would ever want to meet.

At one show, I forgot to bring my boots. All I had was tennis shoes. Back then, it wasn't cool to wear tennis shoes on stage. And J.D. Sumner said, "Son you surely are not going on in tennis shoes?"

I said, "J.D., that's all I've got. I forgot my boots." He asked, "What size do you wear?" When I said, "12", J.D. said, "You have as big a foot as I do." Then he brought me a pair of his boots and I wore them on stage.

After the show, J.D. told me, "They look better on you than on me. You keep 'em'." And I still have them today. I wouldn't take anything for them.

Patsy Andersen – Patsy worked at Graceland for more than two decades. Patsy loves Elvis and loves all Elvis fans. She hired me to do many wonderful things associated with Elvis' great home. I have so many wonderful memories and was able to meet so many great people thanks to Patsy.

Millie Kirkham - Millie Kirkham was another background singer who was so important to that Elvis sound. Millie sang the soprano part on Elvis' "Blue Christmas" and "How Great Thou Art", and so many other iconic Elvis songs.

I was working with the Jordanaires. Millie was retired, but I called her and asked her to do a show or two with us. She had so much fun that she kept working with us until the day she died. She was still out there having a ball when she suffered a stroke and died, just before Christmas of 2014.

Millie smoked like a freight train. She smoked before she went on stage and the moment she got off. When we were in concert, I would also ask Millie "When was the last time you had a cigarette?" She'd say, "Just before I walked on stage." I asked, "What do your doctors think of that?" Millie laughed and said, "My doctors are all dead!"

My love for Miss Millie will never die.

Chapter Thirty

Never Fly Off The Handle

My favorite memory of Millie Kirkham is when we were celebrating her 90th birthday. We were at lunch at Ruby Tuesdays.

She said, "Let me tell you a joke." She said, "Roger Miller told this to me 50 years ago. But I need to stand up to tell it." And she stood up right next to our table in the restaurant.

She said, "There were two buzzards flying around, and they were looking for something to eat. But all they could find was a big pile of cow manure. So they came down and ate and ate and ate. And when they were done, they found they were too heavy to get off the ground. Then they saw an old pitchfork and they climbed it. When they got to the top, they took off and began to fly… but then they both crashed to the ground… graveyard dead."

And Miss Millie said, "So the moral of this story is… Never fly off the handle… when you are full of shit!"

I told that story at her funeral and the entire crowd just went crazy. They fell out of the pews.

With my mother Georgia, 1984

Ronnie, Karen and Tyler

With my wife Karen. Courtesy B.M.I. Archive

Family portrait: Ronnie Dean, Athena, Kara, Ronnie, Karen, Tyler

With Ronnie Dean, Twitty City June 1985 Courtesy June Justice

On stage with Tyler

With Tyler as I am honored at Disney World. Little did I know that I would be a Disney artist 20 years later! Courtesy Walt Disney Co.

With my son Ronnie Dean

With my grandson Ronnie Garon

With my son Craig

My grandson Ronnie Garon at the entrance to Portland Tennessee

Ronnie and J.D. Sumner

On stage with Ed Enoch of the Stamps and J.D. Sumner

With Sun Records founder Sam Phillips. Narvel Felts is on the right

Joe Meador, Iron Eyes Cody, Ronnie. Iron Eyes was the 'crying chief' in the 'Keep America Beautiful' ads

With Mae Axton…the woman who wrote 'Heartbreak Hotel.' I loved Mae.

D.J. Fontana, Ronnie, Scotty Moore. Courtesy Dennis Carney Photo Imaging

Scotty Moore with the car I gave him

With Elvis guitar legends Scotty Moore and James Burton

Ronnie and Scotty Moore

My great friend George Klein. Courtesy Skipper Gerstel

My great friend George Klein. Today

Singing at Graceland Gates

With Louise Smith

With pool legend Minnesota Fats and my manager Don Dortch. I told Fats, "I can't believe I beat you!" He said, "Was there any money on the table son?"

With Country legend Hank Snow

Roy Acuff giving me one of his knives

Ronnie and The Killer Jerry Lee Lewis

Ronnie and Patty Loveless

Tom Jones on the night he told me about showering with Elvis!

Ronnie and Wayne Newton

Ronnie and George Jones. Courtesy Webster PR

Spending Christmas day with George Jones. Courtesy Aaron Crisler

T.G. Sheppard, Ronnie and Bill Medley

Ronnie and T. Graham Brown

Ronnie and Dolly Parton. Courtesy Webster PR

Ronnie and Ray Price

I've always enjoyed getting close to my fans

With Lucille Frye at Tombstone Junction Kentucky

Trick or Treat! I was a scarecrow for a Halloween concert. Courtesy Allen Coker

One of my Christmas For Kids shopping trips

Dear Ronnie McDowell

Thank you for the presents you got me. I like the video game Best. I have the Bandanna on my head, you are so nice. Grandma likes your songs and so does my momma. All the presents are nice. The pretty lady said you bought lots of kids presents at the hospital, you are nice.

Love Amber
13 yrs old

A letter I received from a little girl after our shopping spree

Courtesy Mike Payne

Courtesy Mike Payne

Courtesy Mike Payne

Chapter Thirty-One

Here's Your Sign

One of the biggest honors I've had is when they put up signs at each entrance to my hometown of Portland, Tennessee. The signs say "Hometown of Ronnie McDowell Country Music Recording Star."

I did the "Rick and Bubba" radio show and they teased me, saying "Oh Ronnie, you know you had a post hole digger in the middle of the night and put those signs up yourself!"

You can also cruise down Ronnie McDowell Blvd when you visit Portland. Those honors give me a great deal of pride.

Of all of the things I'm proud of, of course my children come first. But the next thing I'm proudest of is my Cancer Foundation for Children.

I went to St. Jude Hospital in Memphis. I think everyone should visit there, because it will touch your soul. I was so touched that I decided to help in any way I could.

At the same time, one of my dear friends, Ann Thompson, was also looking for a way to help.

I met Ann Thompson in 1999. Her daughter-in-law won front row seats and backstage passes to my show at Renfro Valley Kentucky. And when we met backstage, we just hit it off. Ann started coming to all my shows, and as we started to get to know each other, she told me that her mother, six sisters and a brother had all died from cancer.

And we decided to start a cancer foundation for children. Ann has really done all the work for it. The Ronnie McDowell Cancer Foundation for Children began in 2003. All of the money we raise goes straight to the children and their families. I collect money at my shows, and I sell my clothes at my fan club parties or other events.

We help families with co-pays. We've paid for people's gas to St. Jude in Memphis, or for their medicine. We've paid utility bills for families who have a child with cancer. We've taken toys and gifts to St. Jude. We've donated thousands of dollars to St. Jude.

We've given blankets and other items to Columbus Children's Hospital and to Vanderbilt in Nashville.

Michael's, the arts and crafts store, donated $20,000 worth of merchandise to our foundation, and we took it all to Vanderbilt hospital.

We make gift bags to give to parents who have to stay overnight with their children in the hospital. Each bag has overnight items like combs, toothbrushes and toothpaste.

I have met so many wonderful children through our foundation. There was one little girl who I will never forget. She was five years old. She had cancer. We brought her and her family to Renfrow Valley for one of my concerts. I brought her up on stage and I hugged and kissed her. And she said, "This is the best day of my whole life." She died shortly after that.

We have been able to help and touch so many people. I often wonder about that first time I met Ann when she won that backstage pass. I just know that it was meant to happen. God got us together that night.

If you'd like to make a donation, you can send them to:

Ronnie McDowell Cancer Foundation For Children

PO Box 345

Versailles, KY

Or you can call Ann Thompson at 859-533-8500

My "Christmas For Kids" program is another cause that is very important to me.

Every year, we take 30 underprivileged children out for a shopping trip. I give them $100 each. We have done it for the past 35 years. We take them on a Christmas shopping spree.

Remember that little brown bag of fruit and things I got when I was a little boy at Christmas? Imagine if someone… a stranger, gave you $100 and said, "Go buy whatever you want." Of course back in the 50s, with $100, you could have bought the whole store!

I was in a 7-11 not long ago, and the woman behind the counter said, "Mr. McDowell, you don't know me, but when me and my sister were six and seven years old, you took us on a shopping spree, and that made our Christmas and we will never forget that."

There was a girl one year. She said, "All I want is a new coat." She picked one out and put it on. And she wouldn't take it off. We told her, "You are going to get sick in this hot store with that heavy coat on." But she wouldn't take it off. She was so proud.

I was at the Portland Strawberry Festival, and this beautiful woman walked up to me and said, "Mr. McDowell, I work at Vanderbilt hospital now. I am a nurse. But that shopping trip you gave us when we were little is one of the greatest memories of my life."

I have had numerous people come up to me. They are now grown, in their 30s and 40s, and they thank me for brightening their Christmas many years ago when they were little.

And that really makes all of our efforts, all of our time and money, worthwhile.

Chapter Thirty-Two

The Hits...
And A Couple That Should Have Been

Between 1977 and 1990, I had 34 songs hit the Billboard Hot Country Songs charts. Here are a few thoughts on some of the biggest songs we had:

THE KING IS GONE - Of course, this is the one that really started it all. You just really had to be there to see how fast that song, and my career, totally exploded. And the amazing thing is, it all came from the power of the song itself. I had no manager at the time. I had no publicist. Today you would have a huge team of people pushing the song to radio programmers, and you would have publicists working at getting you publicity from TV and Radio, Newspaper and Magazine interviews. I had none of that! But even though that song was so huge and made such an impact, it still wasn't even a top ten song. Most people think it went to number one. But it only made it to number 13! But that kind of shows you that the charts are not the most important thing. If the people love a song, they don't care where it is on the charts.

I LOVE YOU, I LOVE YOU, I LOVE YOU - I always loved Elvis' song "Hurt". I used that song to get shows in clubs. Me and the band would go in and sing "Hurt", and we would instantly get the gig. I wrote "I Love You, I Love You, I Love You" with "Hurt" in mind. It has that big crescendo ending, and I used to be able to hit that high note with no problem. It's more of a challenge now! One time, J.D. Sumner came up to me and said, "The first time I heard "I Love You", I tried and tried to remember when we did that song with Elvis." Then he realized it wasn't him and Elvis... it was me! This was my first top 5 song.

WANDERING EYES - I had signed with Buddy Killen at Epic. And we searched and searched for a hit. We did a lot of great songs, but nothing would click. But then we heard this song that was written by Jamie O' Hara. Jamie also wrote "Grandpa Tell Me About The Good Ole Days" for the Judds. Jamie played "Wandering Eyes" for me with just his guitar, and I thought "Wow, this is different." That song was unique. There was nothing else like it. It really deserved to go to #1. But it ended up at #2.

OLDER WOMEN - Jamie O' Hara also wrote this. I basically copped and emulated Jamie's version of it, but I did not want to record it. I didn't think that women wanted to be known as older women. I thought it was hard on their ego. But how wrong I was! It was our first #1! And the audience still goes crazy when I sing it.

WATCHING GIRLS GO BY - A top 5 song that is still a favorite for all of my fans. I was listening to the old song, "I'm a girl watcher... I'm a girl watcher...", and I came up the idea and I wrote it. "Watching Girls Go By" has been played over a million times. The beautiful thing about that is, when a song reaches one million plays, the songwriter royalties triple!

I JUST CUT MYSELF - That song almost made it into the top ten. It stopped at #11.

The more I listened to the song, the more I fell in love with it. It really painted a picture. But I had had to convince Epic to put that record out. They said they didn't like the song. Mike Borchetta, Scott's dad, said, "I don't even want to promote that song." But the more the DJs played it, the more people liked it. And it made it all the way to #11, even with very little promotion.

STEP BACK - "Step Back" was written by Craig Morris. He was my piano player for years. He ended up playing for Loretta Lynn. And he went on to form the group Forerunner. "Step Back" was more of a pop song, but Buddy Killen wanted me to do edgier stuff instead of straight country stuff. And that paid off when "Step Back" became a top ten song. We did a music video for "Step Back", and that was the first video that my band, who went on to become The Kentucky Headhunters, were ever in.

PERSONALLY - Karla Bonoff had a huge hit with that song. When I heard it, I thought it would be great for Conway Twitty. So I went to Twitty City and told him about it. But after I left, I thought maybe I should do the song myself. And I did it exactly as I thought Conway would do it. After he heard it on the radio, he said, "I thought you were going to give that to me." I said, "Yeah, I kind of stole your thing." He just laughed.

YOU'RE GONNA RUIN MY BAD REPUTATION - My second #1! Jeff Crossan wrote the song. He was the guy who Conway said, "Don't ever get another song from that boy." This was one time I was glad I didn't listen to Conway. Jeff wrote it as a slow song, a ballad. But I needed an up-tempo record. Me and my band, the Kentucky Headhunters, Greg Martin and Doug Phelps were in Baltimore, and we worked up a fast version of the song and it went to number one. But we actually recorded two versions of the song. We did the slow version, and then the fast version.

YOU MADE A WANTED MAN OF ME - I went back to Jeff Crossan for this one. I thought it had the potential to be a huge record. The lyric was there. Everything was there. It should have been a #1 record. It came very close, but stopped at #3.

I DREAM OF WOMEN LIKE YOU - Conway told me that I needed to meet Troy Seals. Conway said, "He is a great songwriter, and he will write you a number one record". He wrote "Don't Take It Away" for Conway, and he also wrote "Honky Tonk Angel." So I found him, and he said he would send me a couple songs. He sent me a cassette tape that had two songs on it. One was "When We Make Love" that Alabama would record years later. But Troy pitched it to me first, and I turned it down. The other song on the tape was "I Dream of Women Like You." I fell in love with it instantly. And to this day, this is still one of my favorite songs.

I GOT A MILLION OF 'EM - I didn't really want to do that song. The demo was done by my friend, T. Graham Brown. For some reason, I didn't want to do it. But Buddy Killen kept pushing me to do it, and the more I listened to it, the more I liked it. And that was another one of those songs that really should have been a number one song, but it didn't quite make it. It only reached #8.

IN A NEW YORK MINUTE - "In A New York Minute" was written by Holly Dunn's brother Chris Waters, along with Tom Shapiro and Marvin Garvin. They played it for me and the first time I heard it, I thought it was a number one record, and it really should have been. It made it to #5. I still get great response when I do that. A lot of people tell me that it is their favorite song. I love the song to this day.

LOVE TALKS - The group Exile was working with my producer Buddy Killen. Exile's "I Want To Kiss You All Over" is still one of my all-time favorite songs. But Exile switched over from pop to country music, and their producer Buddy Killan was also my producer. He had twenty number one records with them. And I asked them if they would do a song with me. I thought it would be cool if they did all the music and all the harmonies, and they thought it was a great idea. It turned out to be a top ten song.

ALL TIED UP - That song was written on a cold January night. It was snowing up in Mitchellville, Tennessee. My friends Joe Meador and Buddy Killen and I were trying to write a hit song. And I just blurted out "How about 'All Tied Up'?" The melody is unique. It's original. David Briggs, who played with Elvis, played keyboard on the song. When we were in the studio, David came up with this great intro to the song and, as soon as I heard it, I knew we were going to have a big hit. And my favorite line of everything I have ever written is in that song, "Houdini couldn't pull us apart." It was so silly and simple, but that's the favorite thing I've written.

WHEN YOU HURT, I HURT - This was not a big hit. It only reached #37 on the charts. I wrote the song, and I really thought that it was going to be a huge record, and it should have been. But radio was pulling off of me. At that time, I could have recorded the Second Coming and they wouldn't have played it. The radio programmers were coming off of me, and it didn't matter what I did. And that's sad.

IT'S ONLY MAKE BELIEVE - Even though radio was wanting to move on to other artists, I still had one more big hit up my sleeve. And while they might not have played the Second Coming... they were willing to play Conway Twitty. My remake of "It's Only Make Believe" that we turned into a duet with Conway turned out to be a top 5 record for us.

Of course, I wasn't ready for all of my big hits to come to an end, but I am honored that my last huge hit was with my friend Conway.

People always ask me what is my favorite song. And this is it. It is my favorite of everything I've done. Our version was very edgy for the time. The Kentucky Headhunters were on it, but it was Conway who really made it my all-time favorite. And even today on our shows, thanks to today's technology, we are able to play Conway's voice as I sing my part live. And it still gives me chills when I say, "Take it away Conway." And the audience still goes crazy, all these years later.

UNCHAINED MELODY - In 1990, the movie "Ghost" featured the Righteous Brothers' classic "Unchained Melody". Mike Curb came up with the idea of me remaking the song for country radio. I told him, "There is no way I can sing it. Bobby Hatfield is a tenor and I'm a baritone. There's no way I can hit those notes." But Mike insisted I try.

So, a few hours later, I went into the studio. Buddy Killen met me there and agreed to produce the song. As I stepped up to the microphone, I looked up and said "Lord, if you are ever going to let me sing high, let it be today. Because this is the highest thing I will ever try."

And can you believe that we got that song recorded in just three takes?! There was no tuning the vocal back then. You had to sing... and I sang. That is the favorite vocal I have ever done.

Speaking of vocal tuning... if you will listen to every one of my songs, there is no tuning of the vocal. None. I was actually doing the singing.

You had to really sing back then. Today you don't have to sing in tune. Which is stupid. That is the craziest thing. Because you either sing in tune or you don't. I'm glad I grew up in an era when they didn't tune my vocals.

I have had many hits over the years. But there could have been a few more along the way...

I recorded "My Maria" a year before Brooks & Dunn. I had the exact same arrangement and same vocals that Brooks & Dunn did. But Mike Curb and Buddy Killen, my producers, told me, "No, that's too dated. It won't work." When Brooks & Dunn took it to number one, I am pretty sure I told Mike and Buddy, "I told you so."

Chapter Thirty-Three

Didn't You Used To Be...?

I was having all this worldwide success. I was getting gold albums from different countries. I thought when all that happened that it would last forever. We all think that. You finally get what you have been dreaming of, and you think it is going to last forever. But let me tell you this... it does not last!

Gary Brizendine is one of my very best friends. We have been friends since we were five years old. While I dreamed of being a famous singer, Gary dreamed of being a pilot.

We always said when I made it big in music, that Gary would be my pilot and fly me around. And that actually happened. He flew me to my concerts for two or three years.

When my money started rolling in, I hired Gary to be my private pilot, to fly me to all my gigs. I thought I had all the money in the world, but it doesn't last long when you are blowing it like a fool.

I was in my hometown of Portland one day. I was the hottest star going at the time. And there was a man there named David Flemming. He went to school with some of my sisters in the 50s and 60s. David pulled me aside and said, "Ronnie, you need to take some of that money that is pouring in and you need to put some of it away. I know you feel like you are going to be a huge star forever. But it is not going to last forever." I thanked him for his advice, but at the time I was kind of offended. I was like "How dare you tell me my fame is not going to last."

But I recently ran into David, and I reminded him of that conversation. And I told him that I wish to God that I had listened to him.

Chapter Thirty-Four

I'm Going To Disneyland!

You know the TV commercial they make every year with the winning quarterback of the Superbowl? My TV commercial would go something like this…

"Ronnie McDowell, You've been a million-selling country artist for more than three decades… now what are you going to do?"

Ronnie McDowell: "I'm going to Disneyland!"

In the first grade, I drew a big ole red fire engine for my first grade teacher. And I found out I had a talent for art. I got better and better at art through school. And they would have art contests, and some of the kids asked me to draw them something, and they would enter those in the contest! They'd win blue ribbons with a picture I had done.

All of the paintings I do today are like complicated jigsaw puzzles. I love that my children are involved in my painting. My son Tyler Dean comes up with many of the ideas.

I also love the creative process of painting. It is kind of like the creative process of songwriting. With a song, you reach the heart through the ears. With a painting, you reach the heart through the eyes.

The right side of your brain has the arts and entertainment. That includes songwriting, entertaining and singing, and also drawing and painting. And, like my songwriting, I've also grown as a painter and artist over the years.

I have never had a lesson. I love Thomas Kinkade and David Wright, but Norman Rockwell is my favorite. He really painted America.

If you come visit my home, the first thing you will notice as soon as you walk in the front door is a huge mural on the ceiling.

I laid on my back and painted that mural. It is a copy of a Michelangelo. It took me eight weeks. Eight weeks of lying on my back, painting! I put a mattress on top of a scaffolding so I could lay there. The day I finished it was Election Day, and when I signed it, I put: "Obama Elected President" and dated it.

My "Reflection of a King" painting shows Elvis at ten years old looking in the mirror, and he sees his future looking back at him. That painting now hangs at Graceland, and there is another one at Elvis' birthplace in Tupelo.

I also did a similar painting of Oprah Winfrey. It has her looking into the mirror as a young girl, and she is seeing the reflection of herself in the future as the huge TV star she is today. I treasure the handwritten "thank you" note she sent me after she saw the painting. It took me six months to do the Oprah painting, while most of my others take two to three months.

But my life really took a turn after I did a painting of Walt Disney getting on a train. My daughter Athena said, "Daddy, why don't you try to be a Disney painter?"

Something like that was never in my realm of thinking, because they have the greatest artists in the world. But I spent six months on the Disney painting. Then my daughter had a professional photographer come out and take pictures of it. They sent them to Disney Fine Arts and they called my daughter and said, "We want to give your dad a contract."

So in 2013, I went out to Disneyland and signed a 5 year contract with Disney.

I am now doing a series of paintings for Disney. I have to do at least five each year.

They take the originals and sell them in their art galleries. And they take the original art and make prints and Giclees, canvas copies, and they will sell them in the parks and galleries.

CHAPTER THIRTY-FIVE

FRIENDS

I have been blessed to have so many wonderful friends in my life. One hundred books would never have enough pages for me to express my thoughts on all those dear friends. But here are my thoughts on a few very special people:

Joe Meador - I first met Joe Meador at a little music store in Gallatin, Tennessee. Little did we know that we would both travel the world together. Joe did everything for me. He was my manager, road manager, concession man. We wrote songs together. We are still working together. Joe is handling a new publishing company for me. We have been friends for more than 45 years.

In 1990, me and Joe put together a little group called "Six Shooter". The group included my son Ronnie Dean and some young boys we auditioned. And now Ronnie Dean, when he's not playing with me, he's playing with the Coral Reef Band, Jimmy Buffet's band. The little piano player from "Six Shooter", Gabe Dixon, went on to play with Paul McCartney. And Paul thinks he's the greatest piano player he's ever heard.

Joe Meador and I were very close. We still are. Joe's mother had Alzheimer's disease. I asked him if he'd like to go visit with her and sing her some songs. I thought we could sing to the other folks there too. Joe's mom sat there holding Joe's hand as I sang. After that, we started going to different nursing homes. We'd just drop in on them and I'd bring my guitar and play some songs. They didn't know or care if I was a "star". They were just grateful that anyone would come visit with them.

Mike Curb - I was walking down the hall at Curb Records. I had no idea that Mike was a staunch Republican, very conservative. He was a friend and big booster of Ronald Reagan. He was actually the National Co-Chair of Reagan's Presidential campaign.

So guess what my first words to Mike were... I said, "Did anybody ever tell you that you look like one of the Kennedys?" He had that John Kennedy hair. But in spite of that horrible opening line I had, we instantly became the best of friends!

Mike has accomplished so much. He started with nothing and ended up with an empire. And he did it all himself.

He is such a multi-talented guy. He is an unbelievable songwriter. He wrote some of the early hits for Hank Williams, Jr. But not many people know that, when you go to Disney World and you hear that song, "It's a Small World After All"... that is Mike Curb and the Mike Curb Congregation!

No one in the world has been nicer to me than Mike and Linda Curb. Mike Curb believed in me from the very start.

Buddy Killan - Buddy deserves to be in The Country Music Hall of Fame. He is such a pioneer in this business. Buddy Killen and Mike Curb are the two most instrumental people who have helped me in the business. That is the God's truth.

Buddy and I bonded from our very first meeting. We genuinely liked each other. And he became one of my closest friends in the whole world. He was not only my producer, but we were true friends.

Buddy died in 2006, and I miss him every day.

Don Dortch - Don Dortch was one of my best managers. I met Don when he was working with Graceland. He put together shows during Elvis

Week in August. George Klein called Don, and told him he should have me come do some shows in Memphis.

When I did my first sound check there, Don was watching, and he was blown away. He said he couldn't believe what he was hearing when I sang Elvis. And we quickly became very close friends. I didn't have a manager at the time, and I knew Don would do a great job, so I asked him to manage me. We did some exciting things during the time, and even after he stopped managing me, we stayed very close. We still do some concerts together, and we are still great friends today.

Danny Rasberry - I met Danny Rasberry in 1981. He was 24 years old and was promoting his first concert.

Danny chose Ronnie McDowell to be the first show he ever promoted. He also chose an outdoor venue. Just before the show started, a severe thunderstorm passed through, and as the rain poured down, Danny knew there would be no show. Since I was already there, he also knew that he was going to have to pay me. And he knew that his first show was going to be his last, because he was going to lose all of his money.

As I walked up to him, he knew I was going to ask for my check. I can still see his shocked face when I said, "I can come back in two weeks and do the show." He said, "You mean you don't need any money for coming all this way today? No other artist would do that." I said, "Don't worry about it."

Now, three and a half decades later, Danny is still booking me. He has booked or promoted between 100 and 200 of my concerts. If I would have taken his money from that rain out in 1981, Danny would have lost everything. But since I came back two weeks later, we have both been making money for the past 35 years! Imagine how much we have made over those years. If I had been an ass on that first date in 81, we both would have lost out.

By the way, on that first date: when I came back two weeks later, Danny made a huge profit of $45! But that was all he needed, and he was on his way to being a professional concert promoter.

Jim Calloway - One of my best friends through all my life has been Jim Calloway. Jim was in my PE class in high school. He was a senior, and I was a sophomore. But you couldn't tell he was older, because he was one of the smallest boys in school.

While I was always great at all sports, I quickly noticed that they always picked Jim last when we were choosing our teams in PE. And sometimes they would say, "You take Jim and we'll give you a ten point lead."

But I liked Jim, and when I got to be the one to choose our team, I always picked him. And I told them that they could keep their ten extra points!

I didn't really think anything of it, but Jim never forgot that I was kind to him in school. After I got home from the Navy, we ran into each other and we have been friends ever since. Jim has gone on the road with me at times, and we formed a little company where he would make prints of many of the local paintings I would do. I did the original and he made the prints, and we split the profits.

In 2007, a tornado came through Gallatin. It killed Jim's brother, Paul. But Jim has been like a brother to me.

He was small in school, and still is, but Jim went on to become a very big man in Portland. He was even elected mayor. He is an important guy in the community, and in my life.

Charles Wilkinson - Charles and his family have owned the Portland Funeral Home forever.

I would see Charles around town, and at the funeral home, but he would never come to any of my shows.

But one day I saw him in the audience. After the show, I told him I was surprised he was there. He said, "I always thought I was too busy to come see your show. But after my wife passed away, I went out to her car. And when I opened the glovebox, it was full of Ronnie McDowell tapes and CDs. They fell out everywhere. And I didn't even know she listened to you. So I thought I would come see what she liked about you."

After that, Charles started coming to all of my shows. And not only would he come, but he would bring as many people as he could. The last show he was at, he brought fifteen people.

Gary Brezendine - Gary and I both grew up together in Portland. And while I have been able to travel and see the world, Gary has seen even more than I have.

When we were little boys, we lived less than a mile from each other. We were best friends. We would swim all day or ride our bikes to White Oak cave near Portland. I would eat with his family, and he would come to our house and my mother would fix him grilled cheese sandwiches.

Gary became a pilot. He was my private pilot for a few years, but for the last decade he has worked overseas, flying big executives and VIPs in Hong Kong and Saudi Arabia.

I'd do anything for Gary today. If I won the lottery, or if he won the lottery, I'd share it with him and I know he'd share it with me. He'd probably give me more than I would give him!

We were friends growing up. And we are still friends today... even though neither one of us has grown up yet.

Ann Thompson - Ann Thompson runs my Cancer Foundation For Children.

Ann and her husband Charlie have two sons, but she says she has three and I am their oldest. They kind of adopted me years ago.

Ann loves to shop, and she loves to find bargains. She buys me tennis shoes and even underwear! I never know what I will get in the mailbox from her.

Ann is one of the most giving humans I have ever seen. She will call and say, "There is a sale at Kohl's. I'm sending you two new pairs of tennis shoes." She always keeps me in new shoes!

For Christmas, she gives me the exact same things she gives her own sons.

Ann also helps with my Christmas For Kids program. She helps make gift bags to give to each child. Each bag includes caps, gloves, toys and coloring books. She is the most loving person.

And she is a true friend. She will scold me at times. If she thinks I have done something wrong, she'll tell me.

She actually gave me the key to her house. And a funny thing happened when I was there one time. I had let myself in in the middle of the night. A few minutes later, I noticed there was a dog in the living room.

The next morning, Ann and her husband Charlie were cooking breakfast. The dog was laying on the kitchen floor.

When I came down for breakfast, I said, "When did you get a dog?" They both looked at each other and then to me and yelled, "We thought it was yours!" It was a stray dog that had somehow gotten in during the night.

Rex Graves - Rex Graves has been my best friend since we were six years old. We met in the first grade. There's not many people who have had a best friend for 60 years!

We have laughed and cried together. We have shared the highest highs and the lowest lows.

We are honest with each other. If I need him, he is there. And I am there if he needs anything.

When I started having hit songs, I hired Rex to be my bodyguard. He traveled with me for a few years. Rex also loved to sing. He is a good singer, and he has opened for me on a lot of shows.

And he will always be my best friend.

Allen Coker - I met Allen Coker in 1967. He played on the Gallatin High School football team. Of course, I played on Portland's.

Allen always teased me that I never played much football. He always said I only stayed out long enough to get in the team picture and then I would quit!

We met when Portland played against Gallatin. Allen was running the ball. I was wearing number 28, and I tackled him. He got up and said, "Hey, good tackle number 28." I did a double take and couldn't believe an opposing player was giving me a compliment for tackling him.

I knew at that moment that we would become friends. And we have been friends ever since.

In 1976, we ran into each other in a restaurant in Portland. Allen started working on the road with me in 1981. He worked on and off over the past three decades.

Allen ran my concessions on the road. He sold my t-shirts and records for quite a few years. Many of my longtime fans know Allen.

Kathy Meadows - Kathy bought my farm in Portland.

She is one of the most giving humans I have ever known. I know she won't like me sharing this, but I'm going to tell it...

We have been doing my "Christmas For Kids" shopping trip for three and a half decades. And we would not have been able to help so many children without Kathy. She gives us money for those children every year.

It is amazing the people Kathy helps and the things she does. She is the kindest, most generous, loving person in the world.

Rodney and Carolyn Elrod - I wish everyone could have friends like I have in Rodney and Carolyn Elrod. They live in Georgia. They had a club there, and they booked me there years ago. I played them my song "Single Woman". Rodney really liked the song, and he paid to have a professional video done. Rodney and Carolyn also paid for the entire production of one of my gospel albums. They did all that for me, just because they love me. They didn't have to do that.

Larry/Wanda Collins - Larry and Wanda are from my hometown of Portland. They grew up poor, like all of us.

But Larry got into construction... Larry and Fred White, a former mayor of Portland, got together and they helped bring big companies in to Portland. Larry built all those factories, and helped bring lots of jobs into Portland. Larry and Fred also started the Volunteer State Banks in the Portland area.

When I hit it big, Larry asked me to put my money in his bank. I did. And as my career got hotter, every now and then the bank would get a call from someone who wanted to know how much money I had in the bank! A lot of folks are curious about how much money a country "star" makes!

When I was a teenager, Larry and Wanda let me swim in their lake. While I was swimming, a fish grabbed ahold of my left nipple. I got out of the water and that fish was still sucking on my nipple, and when I pulled it off, my nipple started bleeding like a stuck hog! Wanda still remembers that day.

Long before I ever had any hits, Larry and Wanda booked me to sing at parties and events. Then, throughout my career, Larry and Wanda would fly twenty or thirty people all over the country to see me.

Most people have no earthly idea what Larry and Wanda Collins have done for Portland. But Ronnie McDowell knows. They have helped so many people.

Edie Hand - I met Edie Hand more than 20 years ago. She was Elvis' cousin. Her grandmother and Elvis' grandmother were sisters. We became great friends. So great, that we did a book about Elvis together. She used my "Reflections of a King" painting for the cover of the book. She is a great lady.

JoAnn Gore - If you have ever been to a Ronnie McDowell show, there is a good chance you have seen my cousin JoAnn Gore. JoAnn has sold tickets for me and has promoted my shows for a long time. Most of our local shows are always sold out. And a big reason for that is the effort that JoAnn makes to sell those tickets. JoAnn stands only about 3 foot tall, but she is a lot tougher than she looks. I call her Sergeant Carter. She mans the door at all of the shows I do close to home, and she will not let anyone in without paying. And I mean nobody! My best friend Rex Graves was singing on one of the shows with me. He was part of the show, but JoAnn made him pay $25 to get in! The next day, he called me up and said, "I have known you since 1956... and the last thing I am going to do is pay $25 to see your ass... especially when I'm part of the show!"

One time, JoAnn called me and said, "Oh, I am so glad you answered." I asked why. She said someone had just called her and said, "I am so sorry to hear about Ronnie passing away. I didn't even know he had cancer." JoAnn said, "He didn't have cancer and he is not dead!" It turned out that it was the actor Roddy McDowell who had died.

Wink and Sandy Martindale- Sandy dated Elvis when she was 14! Elvis was 25. Wink has done it all. He was one of the first to interview Elvis on TV and then of course he went on to make it huge as a game show host. I recently stayed with Wink and Sandy and we all went to Disneyland. And he rode all the rides with us. He loved the Soarin Around The World ride. Wink is a class act.

I am also thankful for the hard work and friendship of all of my former secretaries. My thanks to Betty Bradley, Lloyd and Ivy Deasy and Rhonda Wright. And my special thanks to my secretary of many years Karen Sherrill. Karen still watches every penny for me.

Chapter Thirty-Six

If Older Women Are Better...
Older Men Need To Stay Healthy!

As I write this book, I am 65 years old. I am not ashamed to tell my age.

When I started having hits in 1977, my image as a "sex symbol" received lots of promotion. 40 years later, it is not easy living up to that "sex symbol" image... but I have always managed to stay physically fit. I am also one of those who says, "You are only as old as you feel." And I feel like I am about 35.

What is my secret to staying young?

If you eat right, if you exercise, and if you keep stress out of your life, you will live longer, you'll look better and you'll feel better.

I also like to hang around younger people. I like to have my kids and my grandkids around me. A lot of your health and fitness has to do with your attitude. I know that one day, Father Time will go "Son, you are old." But I have always had a youthful attitude. I've always enjoyed rollerblading. I played every sport there was when I was in school. I played baseball, basketball, football. I got to where I was a good racketball player. I was always athletic.

When I grew up, I always ate healthy. There was a restaurant in Nashville called "The Laughing Man". I would eat there all the time, and I really got to where I loved healthy food.

It ain't rocket science. That old adage "we are what we eat"... that is so true. If you put a cheeseburger in your mouth every day, you're gonna look like a cheeseburger.

When we were on tour, we used to stop the bus to toss a frisbee or a football. But a lot of my band members, I couldn't get them to join in. They'd rather eat a sack of fries and three quarter-pounders. I had one band member who would order a family meal from Kentucky Fried Chicken, and he'd eat every bit of it himself.

At the age of 65, I started doing P90X, which is very brutal. Everybody thinks that I am insane for doing P90X workouts, but I love it.

I never want to retire. The last thing I want to do is sit on the porch and do nothing. I have no desire to play golf all the time.

I went to see Tony Bennett. Tony was performing in Biloxi. I love him. And at the age of 87, he sounded like a million bucks. And I said right there, "That is what I want to be doing when I'm 87. I want to be standing on a stage somewhere singing, "Older women… are beautiful lovers."

And boy, that will really fit then, won't it?!

I've done everything I ever wanted to do. I've had my day in the sun… and it was as bright as I dreamed it would be. How many people can say that?

Chapter Thirty-Seven

Parting Song
By Scot England

"I never will forget."

I must have heard that 1,000 times over the last six months. It is one of Ronnie McDowell's favorite phrases. And I am so glad that Ronnie McDowell never forgets!

To write a great autobiography, you need a great memory. And that is one of Ronnie's (many) gifts.

On most "star" autobiographies, when you see the word "With" on the cover, that usually means that the name behind the word "With" is the person who really wrote the book. But in this case, it was Ronnie who really was "Bringing It To You Personally."

For six months, I went to Ronnie's home once or twice a week. Each day I would videotape or audiotape him for one to four hours. I just turned on the tape and let him talk. When I say the book is in his own words... it is.

I also had the honor of visiting with many of Ronnie's friends. After they shared their memories, I took those back to Ronnie and used those to jog his memory. Then he gave me his version of those same events.

A couple "behind the scenes" stories about the book...

It is easy when you are talking to someone about their great times, but it's not easy when you have to ask someone to open up about the worst times in their life. No one likes to remember the times they have made mistakes. All of us have things in our life we would like to forget... and we sure wouldn't want the entire world to know about them.

So I had dreaded the day that I would have to ask Ronnie about his divorce. But I knew it had to be done. I also knew this would be the toughest day of our entire book... for Ronnie, and for me. So I had the video camera set up, and I asked him one hard question after another. He answered them all. On my way home, I thought, "Wow, I'm glad that is over. Tomorrow we can go back to talking about funny road stories."

When I got home, I put the video card in my computer and found that I had nothing! I had forgotten to hit record on the camera! I have never felt worse! I almost threw up.

I was supposed to go back for another session this next morning. I thought, "Maybe I will get lucky and just won't wake up. Maybe I will die and won't have to tell him we have to do it all over."

But I woke up. And when I walked into Ronnie's living room the next day, I said, "Ronnie, there's something I need to tell you." He stopped me and said, "Well Scot, I need to tell you something first." He said, "I didn't sleep at all last night. I did some soul searching. And I was not honest with the answers I gave you yesterday. I want to do it all over and tell the truth." I smiled and said, "Well if you insist!"

We both had a huge laugh after I told him what I had done.

One more story… My dad always preached to me about the value of jumper cables.

He always said, "Make sure you have jumper cables in your trunk. You need them there in case you have trouble, or in case someone else needs help."

Dad probably asked if I had jumper cables three or four times a year. By the time I had turned 50, I had still never used those jumper cables. Not once.

But that would change, a few months after Ronnie and I started working on his book.

We had decided to visit Ronnie's hometown of Portland, Tennessee. He would drive me around and introduce me to some of his friends.

But when I pulled up to his home, Ronnie was in his driveway. His car hood was up. I said, "Ronnie, are you having trouble?" He answered, "Hey Scot, you wouldn't have a set of jumper cables, would you?" I said, "You know what… I sure do."

As Ronnie hooked the cables up, I sat in my car and called my father. I said, "Dad, you know those jumper cables you always made me have? You won't believe whose car I am jumping."

That day was one of the highlights of my life. Because I was able to help Ronnie McDowell in that very small way.

I dedicate this book to my best friend, James DeVore. James was the world's biggest Ronnie McDowell fan. James was just 27 years old when he died in 1991.

Before James died, Ronnie called him while he was in the hospital. I never forgot that kindness that Ronnie showed to my best friend.

And now, 25 years later... I am honored to help Ronnie with his life story.

I know that James has been cheering us on as we have put together this book.

We did it James!

I want to thank all of Ronnie's family and friends who welcomed me into their homes. I had the honor of sharing meals and getting to know so many wonderful people.

My sincere thanks to June Juanico, George Klein, Scotty Moore, Jim Ritz, Ray Walker, Louise Smith, D.J. Fontana, Greg Martin, Doug Phelps, Ann Thompson, Barbara Rippy, Gary Brezendine, Rex Graves, Danny Rasberry, Wanda Myrick and Jim Calloway.

My very special thanks to Joe Meador, Allen Coker, Mike Payne and Dennis Carney, for allowing us to use all of your great photos. Thank you to Paula Underwood Winters for helping me keep track of those photos, and for designing the great cover.

To Renae Johnson, thank you for getting me to Nashville... and for all of your help, support and guidance since then. I could not have done it without you!

I thank my biggest fans, my Mom and Dad. You have cheered me on in everything I have done. Thank you for your love and support.

To Jayne... we've come a long way since I played Ronnie McDowell's "Personally" on the radio for you. Thanks for your love, support and prayers over all the years.

Alison, I am so proud to be your Dad.

And most of all, I thank Ronnie McDowell. Thank you, Ronnie, for your friendship and trust. And thank you for letting me be the one who helped you tell your amazing story.

Scot England